Ending Anita

How Two Key West Bartenders Won Gay Marriage For Florida

Anthony Adams

ISBN-10: 0692741887
ISBN-13: 978-0692741887

For Aaron and Lee who improved the lives of all in Florida

CONTENTS

Preface

The Death Of Fabulous

Poolside at *Island House*, Key West's dreamlike gay resort, I am able to forget for a moment the dreadful results of our recent presidential election. Here, men celebrate their sexuality without fear. Here, we are spared the bigotry, homophobia and the renewed threats to the marriage equality victory that is the subject of this book.

Watching the men at play in the *Island House* pool reminds me of another moment of respite from the strife of battling for equality. I was standing on the steps of the Supreme Court in Washington DC with Aaron, Lee and the Key West contingent on April 28, 2015 while the Justices heard oral arguments in the marriage equality case *Obergefell v. Hodges*. That brilliant day made me feel that the relentless controversy of being part of the LGBT community was finally behind me. Despite sharing the hopeful euphoria of the crowd, I had a moment of dread about the victory we all expected. I did not want to relinquish the life I had built. My husband and I had worked hard to overcome personal and professional discrimination, and we were happy with the life we had fashioned for ourselves in an inhospitable world. I wanted to jump up in front of the cheering throng of activists and plaintiffs from around the country and say, "Wait a minute! Are you sure this is what we want? Won't equality mean assimilation? Do we really want to blend in? Do you really want to never feel that flood of relief when you walk into a gay bar with its blackened windows to finally breathe that huge sigh, knowing that for the next few hours you can be yourself? Do you really want to walk about in all this sunlight?"

It was suddenly clear to me that guys like Aaron and Lee are inadvertently killing something that I had come to cherish -- the "fabulous" me and my kind. Aaron and Lee will never fully appreciate the impetus for camp or outrageous style. They won't have that distinctive gay flair, that excruciatingly fine taste, that need to talk fervently about the catalogue of a wartime chanteuse. They won't ever feel compelled to collect Depression glass, dammit! The gay generations to come will be the children of Huntsman and Jones, and my children as well, but when they open their mouths to speak or as they walk down the street, they will be indistinguishable from the world around them. They will not be fabulous.

There was a day, not too long ago, when men were identified as gay primarily because they had a certain style. The suave ascot, the right furniture, the perfect hair, that sweater and the clever turn of a phrase proclaimed that which could not otherwise be spoken. In the 20th century, most folks did not recognize the special accent that was the essence of gay expression, while we who were seeking our gay tribe seemed, by instinct, to hear it in the wind. Straight and closeted America shared the same songbook, but only we who sought the other side of the rainbow understood the subtext. In a world that shunned us, we remained masked men whose only relief from the exhausting work of hiding our sexual selves was our stylish expression. We made you laugh. We made you gorgeous. We tried to make you love us without ever seeing us. We were fabulous for ourselves and for you.

In its extreme, gay male stylishness became laborious, fetishistic, embarrassing and ultimately rueful. At its best, it was how America celebrated itself in song, story and image. Its fundamental message was often laced with a pervasive sadness. Gay men fully understood the bitter desperation of Blanche Dubois, the defiance of Joan Crawford, and above all else, Dorothy's desire to find home. Gay stylishness was rooted in a predicament, the need to overcome the odds of a deck stacked against us. We had no choice but to distract the players with our flair.

When I launched myself as a closeted gay man in the 1970s, I didn't need to be told that Cole Porter, Truman Capote and Paul Lynde were my godfathers. I knew that I was of their tribe, and that it was my responsibility to take what I could from their example. I felt called to use their script in order to take my place as an inventive, productive and shining member of that larger world which had only the slightest suspicions about my hidden truth. At the breakfast table of my boyhood, I had already learned to receive praise for the amazing painting I had produced or report I had written for school, while also silently enduring occasional words from my parents or siblings deriding "the queers." I did not quite know what the word meant but I had a sickening feeling that I would become one. I fused my ability to please people with my sense of style and my growing sense of secret queerness.

Oddly, I did not abandon the deceit of style when I stepped into my first gay bar! On the contrary, I perfected it through a succession of personae. I entered "Uncle Charlie's Midtown" in New York City wearing glossy red-rimmed glasses, Calvin Klein jeans, red Converse Chuck Taylor sneakers and a full-length nutria fur coat from Saks 5th Avenue's Revillion Boutique. Within a year, I was appearing in nothing but plaid flannel shirts (with the sleeves ripped off) and work boots. This gave way to a completely disturbing line of black leather, which was replaced by a drab olive military wardrobe extensive enough to have taken Grenada. At work, my elegant 3-piece suits got me promotions. (There had also been a few strange but significant years in which I glided about the Vatican in a black serge cassock made by the pope's private tailor.) I began to relish the fact that I could step out of myself to become any one of the Village People - or none of them - at the drop or the lift of a hat. Now, I look at my closet from the outside. If I am to be equal, and if I am to be assimilated, I'll have to throw out a lot of finery.

The 21st century arrival of the "visible gay" put an end to the need to be fabulously stylish and gave birth to gay assimilation. Now, I am wearing ratty slippers when I step out of my suburban house to see my husband off to work, giving no thought to what I may be wearing. I greet the neighbors and we talk about our gardens over the fence. They don't compliment my clothing because it is unstudied and identical to their own. Gone is the assumption that acceptance of gay culture would mean ratcheting up our need to be stylish to almost unsustainable levels. Actually, the opposite occurred. I don't check my hair before I go to the grocery store. I don't apply a skin lifting/firming lotion to my face before I go to the gym. *I* am visible. I celebrate the person I am rather than those characters I used to play when I could not be me. I still have some style, but only when I want it and never because I need it as an antidote to oppression.

Were we prepared for this side effect of the winning of our equal rights? I was not. I had not realized how much my "fabulousness" was due to my status as closeted and/or unequal. Now that it is gone, I find myself missing it. At a meeting of the board of directors of my condo association in south Florida, of which I am a member, it was announced that my husband would be assisting with the association's replacement of the sign on the front of our building. (He owns a sign design and manufacturing company.) He was not referred to as my friend or companion. There was no awkward skirting of a descriptive. There was no hushed tension. This is what it means to be equal and assimilated. I am glad for it, but I miss the old days when our relationship had a darkly fantastic quality to it that was far from mainstream or pedestrian. We were exotic in a thrilling way. We were our own special creations, as goes the song.

How we got to a time and a place in which a gay man would enjoy the easy luxury of visibility over stylization is the prelude to the story of Aaron Huntsman and William Lee Jones, two very visible and real men of Key West whose demand for marriage equality resulted in the reversal of Florida's anti-gay laws prohibiting same-sex marriage -- laws spawned by Anita Bryant's homophobic campaign of 1977.

Aaron and Lee have been "Conchs" (residents of Key West) for many years. Born elsewhere, they are "Freshwater Conchs." (The designation "Saltwater Conch" may be claimed only by someone who is native.) They fit perfectly in a town that once proclaimed its independence (April 23, 1982) because of an annoying Federal border patrol roadblock. The "Conch Republic" may have been brief and less than serious, but the pride and maverick playfulness that spawned it still thrive. The official Key West slogan "One Human Family" is no joke. There may be no other place in the USA where straight and gay residents mix so fervently in their desire to rub shoulders, toast each other, wear and share sequins and plumes, and slap each other's butts with audacious catholicity.

Aaron and Lee are bartenders at two prominent gay bars on Duval Street, but their clientele is a homogenous mix of locals and tourists of every persuasion. In Key West, bartenders are like bishops tending their flocks by dispensing the spiritual sustenance of a good drink. They know what is happening in their town and are well-informed about the status of the battle for gay rights in other states and around the world. As would any true Conch, Huntsman and Jones became irritated over the fact that they would have to travel out of state in order to marry each other. They wondered why Florida was dragging its feet in the struggle for marriage equality. The docile acceptance of onerous and unjust prohibitions is simply not in the DNA of a Conch. Nor is acceptance of the premise that they would have to wait patiently for some unspecified future date when Florida's LGBT advocacy groups including *Equality Florida* might or might not decide to push for marriage equality in Florida.

Huntsman and Jones became increasingly frustrated as they watched marriage equality become legal in many other states, while Florida took, what seemed to them, an inactive and wait-and-see approach. They decided to take action without ever having done anything remotely similar and without any training or experience in activism or politics. The fact that they are two blue-collar workers who initiated their protest without the encouragement or support of LGBT advocates or political machinery makes their marriage equality victory in Florida unique.

This is the story of how Aaron Huntsman and William Lee Jones achieved the unimaginable by walking into their County Clerk's office and requesting a marriage license. Theirs is the story of two clearly visible gay men in love. Have they, like me, shed some style in the process of winning marriage equality? No. Their style is modern, smart, loveable, and, above all else, pure Conch. When I bemoan the death of my fabulousness, they try to understand what I am talking about, but their experience is quite different. Both Aaron and Lee were born *post-Stonewall!*

A pompous or somber historical book about the victory of Aaron and Lee would not be appropriate. Pomposity is what you do when you build a mausoleum for those who take themselves too seriously. Aaron and Lee do not take themselves too seriously. They laugh often and loudly. In fact, I got the first and best clue about their personalities when I woke up in the fourth floor bedroom of the Washington DC home of Dan Bready and Kevin Dickinson on the morning of the first day of our trip to demonstrate before the Supreme Court during the hearing of the Obergefell marriage equality case. (Dan and Kevin had graciously offered to host the entire Key West contingent at their home which had at one time been a Roman Catholic priests' residence.) I was awakened by the sound of loud shouting that seemed to come from just outside my windows. When I opened a window and looked down to the courtyard behind the house, I saw Aaron, Lee and their close friends Susan Kent, MiKey Hudson and Mark Ebenhoch having breakfast. There was no emergency, alarm or argument. They were just having a spirited conversation at the decibel level that is ordinary for bartenders and their patrons. I closed the window thinking that these people were a very loud tribe. I soon found out that behind their boisterous words were warmth, sincerity and a passion for justice that infused everything they did. They were also clearly folks who enjoy a good time. I knew that if I was going to write about their marriage equality victory correctly, I would have to introduce them to you in a way that would make you love and respect them as much as do I. A monumental and purely factual approach would not do. You would have to meet them as did I, with their drinks and cigarettes in hand, drowning each other out with the noise of their own laughter and fiercely cherishing each other with deep and protective loyalty.

I also realized that, in telling their story, I had to disclose (with their permission) their status as HIV-positive men. There is a widespread misconception that HIV-positive men go to gay destinations like Key West to find a perpetual happy hour in which to sunset before they wither and die. That is not true of the men who ended Anita Bryant's Florida. Rather than be stigmatized and marginalized, these men, while not averse to happy hours, are productive, thoughtful and inventive citizens who refuse to consider themselves disadvantaged or in any way unqualified to be frontline gladiators and leaders in the fight for equality. They seem by nature to be the opposite of lazy. My admiration for these men and their friends could not be deeper.

On that day in Washington DC, I was not sure if I wanted any child of mine to pass through this world looking, sounding and acting like everyone else, and empty of the need to be fabulous as a way of creating a special world within a hostile and unwelcoming one.

These worries faded as I watched Aaron and Lee openly embrace on the steps of the Supreme Court beneath the billowing rainbow Pride flag they brought to DC from Key West. This is better than suffering the persecutions of Anita Bryant. Depression glass collects dust. Freedom doesn't. The kids will find their own fabulous, and we'll have Aaron and Lee to thank for it. This is the story of how they went from being blue collar bartenders to brilliant activists, and how they won marriage equality for Florida.

INTRODUCTION

I had arranged a November 16, 2015 afternoon meeting with Aaron Huntsman, Lee Jones, Mark Ebenhoch, Susan Kent and MiKey Hudson. We would convene on Duval Street in Key West at the "Back Bar" in the courtyard of *Aqua Nightclub*, where Aaron tends bar. Owner Kimball Ingram graciously offered to host our meeting at his establishment.

This may have been a brilliant idea or perhaps a disastrous one. That is what I was wondering, three drinks into our enjoyable time together. My intention was to listen while they told me the real story of how they hatched their plan to win marriage equality for Florida. The hours we spent together were great fun. Afternoon stretched into evening, and if I incorrectly report some of the details of what they said, you should understand that their own memories about who first had the idea, and who said or did what are fuzzy and often contradictory, as was my handwriting while they spoke. In the course of that delightful session, I gave up trying to make sense of the specifics of their story and allowed myself to enjoy the fierce passion with which they tell it. That passion for equality is the essence of their shared story.

Keep in mind that until the LGBT community became visible to straight friends, neighbors and relatives, many of our would-be allies saw only the theoretical closet and not

1

their loved ones fearfully trapped inside it. Likewise, until you meet and come to love this group of Key West friends, their marriage equality victory is just a political headline.

Who are Aaron, Lee, Mark, MiKey and Susan? The chapters assigned to each of them in this book will be an intimate introduction to them, because you cannot understand the battle for marriage equality unless you clearly see the faces of its soldiers. The essential ingredient of marriage equality is *visibility*.

Aaron is tall and Hollywood-handsome. His rich baritone is stage-worthy. His looks and winning personality will make you want to vote for him should he ever choose to run for some public office. I fear that even though he would be a better leader than many of those whom Florida has endured in recent years, his honesty, and his naive trust of even those who want only to take advantage of him would make him painfully vulnerable in the political arena. With a skilled team to assist him, he might serve well in public office. For the moment, I am glad he's pouring our drinks.

Aaron's husband Lee (William Lee Jones) is a strapping man of the variety that does not set off your gaydar. He is nobody's stereotypical gay. He reminds me of the young Spencer Tracy, but weren't there rumors that both Tracy and his girlfriend Kate Hepburn were gay? Like Tracy, Lee isn't immediately warm and fuzzy with strangers, but once he is comfortable with you, his giggle replaces the gruff demeanor, and is a great reward. A man of few words, Lee is the one I turn to if something the others say in the course of this evening seems incredible or puzzling.

Mark Ebenhoch has the upright stance of a former Marine

and a neck that snaps back at any affront that smacks of insincerity or deceit. He does not tolerate much nonsense and his loyalty runs deep. If he says he's going to be somewhere, you can count on it. He rolls his eyes at Aaron's childlike trust and Lee's reticence. He makes many proclamations in the absolute, but he is not above changing his opinion when contrary information comes his way. Once I learned the complete history of the *Huntsman v. Heavilin* case, I began to wonder if it might not have succeeded without the discipline Mark brought to the team.

MiKey Hudson is the short guy in this tall group. Like Mark, he is dogged in his loyalty to Aaron and Lee but he is more the yappy Chihuahua to Mark's Doberman. Always ready to be let off the leash when something needs to be said to clear the air, MiKey doesn't mince words. Like Aaron and Mark, he will talk nonstop – or at least until Lee gives him a glare that makes him fall silent. It is very easy to excuse MiKey's theatrically exaggeration of his part in each episode of the saga. He is extremely proud to have been a part of their victory. He was Best Man at the wedding of Aaron and Lee. That tells you all you need to know about his place in their lives.

Susan Kent is the tall and voluptuous female force of nature who gives the team balance and articulation. Her radiant smile gives it brilliance and her immense heart gives it passion. When I listened to her tell me the story of the love of her life, I began to wonder if she would ever again know love like that. It will take a very strong and wonderful woman to win the sharp and wise Susan Kent. Is she out there somewhere? I hope so. Meanwhile, I am glad for her witty words delivered with a toss of her lush salt and pepper hair.

When you put this group on barstools, their accounts are full of arguments, disagreements, laughter and repeated attempts to shut each other up so that each could make some point that is important to him or her. By the end of the evening, I knew I had received their truth in a way that transcends the narrative facts presented elsewhere in this book. As I carefully walked back to my room at Island House after so many drinks, I wondered if I would remember much of what they said. I did. Love, passion, anger, friendship and commitment don't fade in the light of morning.

Please keep in mind that because this introduction provides what was said in the course of that jovial meeting, it would be wrong to take any statement out of context and to compare it to something contradictory elsewhere in this book. For the more reliably factual account of what transpired in the course of the *Huntsman v. Heavilin* suit, see the included *Timeline* which I have devised, and also the included court documents and transcripts.

Aaron Huntsman, adding cranberry juice to vodka with the skill of a seasoned bartender, describes trying to get other couples interested in bringing suit against Florida's ban on same-sex marriage, a suggestion made by his lawyers. He says it was not easy to assemble a team. He is still somewhat bitter about the fact that couples initially on board bowed out, but Aaron's lawyers eventually saw more merit to representing just one couple. He and Lee came to see that they would do this on their own. He pauses to show me what he posted on Facebook on February 23, 2014: "Please let me know if there are any other Florida couples that would like to join Lee and I on challenging

Florida's Marriage law. We have our first meeting this Friday at 10AM. Legal counsel has been hired. Please get back to me as soon as possible." Aaron says there were two group meetings with potential plaintiffs. Legal counsel attended those meetings and came to see the merits of working exclusively with Aaron and Lee.

MiKey (who spells his name to emphasize his status as a KeyWester) interrupts Aaron to remind him that they had been talking about it for months before that post went up because he and Aaron did not want Florida to be the last state in the union to get gay marriage. They looked at what they called the "huge gay demographic of south Florida" and were convinced that Key West should take the lead. Aaron responds to MiKey saying, " That's true, but Lee and I had been talking about being officially married since our commitment ceremony in Vegas on our first anniversary. We were treated rudely at the first chapel we chose in Vegas, so we picked a different one that was gay-friendly. That experience of being treated badly really troubled us." Aaron explains that that the experience of being mistreated by an anti-gay wedding chapel in Vegas planted the seeds of activism in their hearts.

Back in Key West and beginning to form a strategy with his lawyers, Aaron became aware of *Equality Florida's* search for couples willing to bring suit for marriage equality in Florida. *Equality Florida* – www.eqfl.org - is the 501(c)(4) organization dedicated to "securing equality and justice for Florida's Lesbian, Gay, Bisexual and Transgender community." Throughout this book, the relationship between *Equality Florida* and the Huntsman/Jones team will not always be portrayed as harmonious. I have chosen to present the perspective of the teammates rather than colorize the relationship to cleanse it of acrimony, repair misperceptions or amplify the turf-war that became part of their mutual desire for marriage equality. Readers are free to further research who did what and why, and to form their own conclusions about the merits or demerits of either group.

Aaron thinks that *Equality Florida* may have interviewed 1200 couples before they settled on six to form the core of their own suit. He began a similar process in Key West, but with some significant differences. Aaron says he felt that *Equality Florida* was looking for a very specific type of plaintiff: scrubbed, professional, mainstream, financially successful and owning businesses that might be useful to them. He knew he would never meet those criteria but that did not stop him from moving ahead with his own case. Through a friend and frequent patron at his bar, he had secured the lawyer he needed. While at his bar and listening to Aaron describe his desire to sue for marriage equality, the friend dialed Attorney Bernadette Restivo and handed the phone to Aaron. Within 24 hours, the lawyers of Restivo, Reilly & Vigil- Fariñas made the trip from Key Largo to Key West and decided that Aaron and Lee were the couple they had been looking for. These lawyers had already become convinced that marriage equality in Florida was something they wished to champion. Aaron's talk over the bar with his friend was serendipitous. The time and place were right. The team began to come together.

Aaron and MiKey remember tracking what *Equality Florida* was up to and closely following the words and actions of Florida Attorney General Pam Bondi because they wanted to successfully introduce their own case in Monroe County to have maximum impact in Florida. Aaron says, "We knew what *Equality Florida* was doing because our attorneys and theirs were working together. It didn't start out as a race between us and them. I just felt that the national and state advocacy groups were dragging their feet, playing some kind of wait-and-see game. I didn't want Florida to end up in the dust. I kept posting on Facebook everything I heard, read and discovered about what was happening. I learned about Florida's "Sunshine laws" that demand transparency. Bernadette would call me up and say, 'Why are you posting all that online?' I think it may have helped the two groups cooperate, at that time anyway."

Aaron and Lee's intent to sue became public before *Equality Florida* formally commenced its suit as the first to file. Aaron and MiKey remember those days in terms of a friendly and cooperative neck-and-neck race between their case and *Equality Florida* but they are careful to add that Bernadette Restivo did not want her *Huntsman v. Heavilin* suit to be at odds with what *Equality Florida* was doing. She felt that the two sets of plaintiffs could be helpful to each other and could progress apace. Aaron says, "I think both groups began to see that it didn't matter whose case won as long as one of them did. *Equality Florida* was helpful to us, and I think they considered us their back-up suit in case theirs failed."

With the lawyers on board, Aaron and Lee became more energized and also increasingly watchful of what *Equality Florida* was doing in Miami-Dade County, and what their plan of action might be in Monroe County, encompassing the Florida Keys. Throughout the entire process, there existed between the two camps an uneasy graciousness signaled by air kisses exchanged at fundraisers and public statements of mutual admiration, but each team wanted to be first out of the gate. While both teams would swear they were not in competition with each other and were working cooperatively for the same goal, it seems obvious that each had a proprietary sense of the value of a headline and the timeliness of their actions.

Mark Ebenhoch jumped into the conversation at this point and attempted to clarify how they actually decided on the date for filing suit. One of the group had received a 3AM call from a friend saying that *Equality Florida* planned to bring seven couples down to the Monroe County Courthouse on April 11, knowing that their chances in Monroe County, a liberal entity, were good, and coinciding with a planned *Equality Florida* gala in Key West. Someone had tipped off *Equality Florida* that Aaron and Lee intended to file on April 14. Aaron, Lee and Mark were on the phone to Bernadette at 3:40AM insisting that their suit happen in advance of that date. They all agreed to hatch their plan on Monday, April 1st.

Aaron remembers this as an extremely stressful time. He began to distrust even close friends whenever information about his suit that should have been confidential became known. He took down his Facebook page and whenever anyone asked about the suit, he would respond that, at the advice of counsel, he could not discuss it.

The fact that Aaron and Lee would be asking the county clerk for a marriage license on April Fools' Day became a source of argument. Aaron thought it would add an amusing note to the proceedings. Aaron says there was another reason for choosing that date, "We kept the date a secret until the morning we filed. I felt that filing on April 1st, the day after the *Equality Florida* gala in Key West would be the last day anyone would have guessed we would be filing. I'm sure their hangovers kicked in that morning due to the news! Months later I was told that certain *Equality Florida* staff were daily calling my co-workers, trying to get info about my plans. I felt paranoid at that time, not trusting my own so-called friends or co-workers. It turns out that I was right to be suspicious!"

At this point, Lee, who had been quietly listening to the others tell their versions of the story from their barstools, entered the conversation. He had wanted their suit to be taken seriously. He did not think showing up at the courthouse to demand a marriage license on April Fools' Day would be helpful. But believing that the actions of others might outpace them, he agreed to the date. It remained important to Lee that their suit not be considered a joke.

Aaron and Lee were worried that *Equality Florida* might get wind of their plans and try to file suit in Monroe County before them. Bernadette warned them to discuss the plan with absolutely no one outside a very tight circle of trusted friends. Before dawn on April 1, 2014, a friend of Aaron and Lee was at the County Clerk's office to warn the couple if *Equality Florida*, or any media arranged by them, should appear. With the coast clear, Aaron and Lee went to the Monroe County Clerk's Office to apply for a marriage license. They were politely declined by the staff at the counter. When Aaron and Lee requested the official application form that would bear an official stamp of denial, they were refused! This was unacceptable and they announced their refusal to leave the premises without it. This sent the staff scurrying into a back office to alert County Clerk Attorney Ron Saunders to the possibility of some unpleasantness. Saunders came forward to greet the couple warmly – Key West is a small town in which everyone knows everyone – and to explain that he really wished the laws were otherwise but that he was unable to grant them a marriage license. He did find a way to give them something in writing. Aaron says, "Attorney Ron Saunders handed me the legal sheet explaining the Florida statute that forbids same-sex marriage. I asked him to stamp it or sign it and he said no. Ron is now running against Amy Heavilin for County Clerk. How ironic is that! We had our friends sign the form witnessing that it had been issued to us in denial of a marriage license."

Within five minutes of leaving the courthouse, Aaron and Lee were on the phone to Bernadette who filed the suit that same day.

At this point, Susan Kent entered the conversation. She had known Aaron since the days when they worked together on the Sea-to-Sea rainbow flag project (June 15, 2003) and had been following his recent Facebook posts about his plans to demand a marriage license. Susan says, "I had a lot of experience with social media and event planning. It became obvious to me that Aaron was going to need a strong team. I offered him my help, saying, 'I can play well with others. I'll help you out with this.'" Aaron adds that he met both Susan and Lee on June 10, 2003, saying, "I met two angels on the same day."

When I asked the group if anyone at that time discouraged them from proceeding with the lawsuit, Aaron said that his mother had misgivings. She had been and still is a court reporter and knew how legal struggles can impact a person's life. She was worried that the fight her son had in mind would tear him apart and she did not want anything bad to happen to him. Aaron and his mother had this conversation only two days before the filing, so Aaron simply assured her that he could manage it. He reminded her that he would use his theatrical training and she came around. Aaron says, "I reminded her of the enormous media contacts I had acquired over the years in gay Miami beach and as a bartender. Also, all the associations I had in the LGBT community in Florida, California, Nevada and New York. I was ready to take this case on. I had already been 'on stage' for years in public working as a bartender, model and actor. This wasn't anything new to me. Now she is very proud of what I have accomplished."

No one in Key West advised them against proceeding with the suit. Aaron and Mark said there was the usual jealousy and gossip and petty back-stabbing that comes to anyone who actually does something rather than just talk about it, but they didn't mind. They understood that their actions would be processed in a political context and that their Key West community is comprised of both Democrats and Republicans who would feel the political charge of their action differently. They also considered the impact of their actions on the allies and members of *Equality Florida* who were based in Key West and were their friends and bar patrons. They knew there would be some abrasion as the two initiatives moved forward competitively, but they were confident that ultimately real friendships would endure any disputes.

The assembling of funds and the accrual of media coverage were areas that needed the team's focus. They knew *Equality Florida* would be capable of using its infrastructure to raise funds for their plaintiffs. On the other hand,

Aaron, Lee and their team would have to proceed with the pro bono help of their lawyers and no financial resources. This did not bother them in the slightest.

Once the filing happened, Aaron remembers that everything seemed to go into high gear as the media inquiries became a barrage. This evening, on their barstools, as they tried to remember who contacted whom, it became clear that some of them remember contacting radio, press and TV, while others remember being contacted by media without doing any outreach. Aaron says, I was inundated by the media. I met Mark on July 17th, the day after the ruling on our case. I gave Mark all the media contacts I had been working with and also had cultivated because of this case. Mark brought in his own talents and contacts and married them all together and managed it all. I was so happy he joined us as we all were so overwhelmed. Mark had multiple years of media experience as a military adviser on many blockbuster Hollywood movies."

Mark says he sent out media advisories that generated the significant interest. On Facebook, Aaron continued to document the media coverage of their suit. It became clear that viewers, readers and listeners the world over were going to follow the two bartenders who would not take no for an answer to their request for a marriage license. Their action was soon understood to be no joke. They were serious plaintiffs with a savvy team and excellent lawyers, all of whom were passionate about marriage equality.

At this point, MiKey reminds us all that from that time on, he was convinced they would win. He says, "I kept saying over and over again, 'We got this! We got this!'" When

MiKey says "win," he is not referring to winning a race; he is referring to the justice and equality that the team sought for everyone in Florida. Aaron adds, "The case was going forward at lightning speed. With the help we were getting from multiple law firms, and based upon the demographics of Monroe County, we were sure this case would not be pushed under the rug or dragged out. This is what we had always thought. We didn't know if we would be heard first or last, win or lose, but if we could make a difference in just one gay person's life, this whole experience would be worth all the time we had invested. It was no longer about having *our* victory; it was about having a part in all the Florida cases."

Susan remembers that Aaron was relatively naïve about social media even though he had a strong base. She says he did not know how to create a hashtag or the rules of hashtag etiquette. He learned fast, and with Susan and eventually Mark guiding them, Aaron and Lee handled their interviews brilliantly. It became suddenly apparent that if, as Aaron suspected, it had been true that *Equality Florida* preferred plaintiffs who were professionals, financially secure, polished, and equipped with children or careers that "fit in," they had miscalculated the strength of the two very convincing, lovable and sincere Key West bartenders. [As an aside, I'd like to clarify that I have never received input from *Equality Florida* about how they selected the couples they chose to be their marriage equality champions. I have not asked *Equality Florida* if they recall considering Huntsman and Jones for the team and if so, what may have been their reasons for choosing others.] Susan says, "I hit on the 'two regular guys' angle right off the bat, and at first, Aaron and Lee were a little bit uncomfortable with it. They hesitated to embrace that reality because we all have this vision of the ideal and convincing plaintiff who is the shining emblem of assimilation. The beauty of marketing these two was that unlike a non-profit like *Equality Florida*, for instance, we didn't have to market them to any specific demographic. We didn't have to meet any goals or work within any parameters. If someone turned up a nose at the thought of two gay bartenders, it didn't matter. We didn't have to script them or shape them."

To be clear, the group tells me that *Equality Florida* celebrated and congratulated Aaron and Lee on their filing almost immediately. In the weeks to come, that assistance often took the form of leaving their brochures at events hosted by Aaron and Lee or trying to collect funds for *Equality Florida* from guests who had come to events hosted by Aaron and Lee. Aaron says, "The events we did were fundraisers for our law firm, not for us. We were never reimbursed for any costs we had accrued. Not even one dollar. At one point we had taken so much time off work and were doing so many fundraisers, we became late with our own bills. We went through all our savings. We are still trying to catch up financially years later. We did get a $1000 contribution from Metropolitan Community Church of Key West to defray legal expenses, and we were awarded a $1000 humanitarian grant. We were very private with our finances. We didn't want people to know our financial circumstances, and we were too embarrassed to ask for help. We feel special gratitude to Reverend Steve Torrence and Joan Higgs for reaching out to us in a time of need. We still have not officially had the money for a real honeymoon."

In thinking back on those fund-raising events, the team says that they came to understand that *Equality Florida's* fundraising in Key West depends largely on snowbirds who may have the mistaken notion that the money they donate is used for the LGBT community of Key West. Many of those who gave money to *Equality Florida* at events hosted by Aaron and Lee may have thought they were giving financial support to the couple when they were actually supporting *Equality Florida's* statewide work. I do not know how to assess the veracity of this opinion but the team feels strongly about this. They do not begrudge *Equality Florida* its successes in Florida but they were not and are not about to allow any person or group to ride the coattails of what they have accomplished. In my interview with MiKey, you will find specific accounts that support the lessons they learned about how *Equality Florida* operates in Key West.

Aaron is shaking his head in agreement while Susan talks. Glasses are raised and clinked and refilled. Aaron remembers that *Equality Florida*, seeing the media attention he and Lee were getting started calling him up and suggesting that they arrange and host interviews for the couple. Aaron says he began putting them off with excuses such as a toothache or a cold. Aaron says that the last thing he wanted at that point was to be molded into something useful for someone else's objectives. He says he did consent to an interview with the national LGBT advocacy group *Freedom To Marry*, and that *Equality Florida* cut and pasted the resultant story on their own website using photos without attribution.

At this point Lee, who had begun to do a slow burn during the discussion of media coverage, spoke up. Ordinarily quiet, he expressed anger about the way Aaron, Mark, Susan and MiKey were describing those days. He said, "You are all making it seem as if we were in it for fame and notoriety. Let's keep that stuff in perspective." Duly noted by all, but they had much more to tell me about the days immediately following the filing of their suit.

Aaron remembers that soon after they got denied the license and filed the suit through Bernadette, the phones were ringing off their hooks, and he began to feel that the entire situation was moving beyond his control. He knew the momentum would not last unless he did something to "bring things up a notch." He decided that what was needed was a local Key West rally. They marched in the July 4th parade in Key Largo, and they decided to stage a July march down Duval Street in Key West.

Aaron remembers the unfolding of their staged events at that time, saying, "Bernadette said her law firm was being badly impacted financially by the huge number of hours they spent pro bono on our case, and would I put on some fundraisers. We did a meet and greet at the *801* upstairs at the cabaret during Pride. We did a fundraiser at the *Bottle Cap* following our ruling. We did a fundraiser at *Salt Fusion* in Tavernier fearing we were headed to the Florida Supreme Court and that would entail more legal expenses. State Representative David Richardson and members of *SAVE-Dade* drove from Miami and were joined by State Representative Holly Reich Raschein giving $5,000. I came up with multiple rallies in front of the County Clerk's Office before our court date to bring media awareness on a local, state and national level. Lee got us the meet-and-greet location at the *801* with the owner's blessing. I came up with the idea of a sign-making party before our court date. I called the *Human Rights Campaign* and *Equality Florida* and had them send me signage knowing that if we had media present that their signage would stand out. Susan frowned at this idea but I did it anyway. I came up with the idea of a marriage theme in the Gay Pride event for the bars and city. This was the best Pride Key West had seen since the "Rainbow 25 "event with the Sea-to-Sea flag in 2003. After the sign-making party, we marched down Duval Street and back with the help of *Real Events Key West* and local radio's *Rude Girl* announcing our march for days. Other local radio stations were also interviewing me and calling for the city to come together in support of what we were doing. Susan handled the fundraising portion of the events by getting multiple Key West businesses to donate gifts for raffles and silent actions. I coordinated the Florida newspapers, radio, news-stations, and reporters. Susan handled the local publications. All the media work was handed to Mark following the historic July 17th ruling.

Whenever Aaron contacted the media outlets in Miami and Fort Lauderdale, they readily agreed to come down to Key West to cover these events. Says Aaron, "They love coming down here anyway because, hey, it's Key West, so there was no problem getting them here. So *HRC* sent us some material as did *Equality Florida* and we figured that it didn't matter who marched with us. We wanted everyone to be united behind the idea of marriage equality. We opened the door to anyone. With our new so-called 'endorsements,' we thought the law firm would get more than just legal help. We thought they might get some financial help. This is why we used signage from HRC and *Equality Florida*. This never happened."

At this point, the team was assisted by Shannon Cubria Farris who was editor of *Real Events Key West*. He began to offer media help with what became the team's official umbrella *LoveIsLoveKeyWest*, the local expression of the international #*loveislove* campaign. Shannon and his husband Joe would accompany the team to Washington DC for the demonstration on the steps of the Supreme Court during the Obergefell hearing that eventually toppled all the state bans on same-sex marriage and made marriage equality the law of the land. Aaron says, "*Freedom To Marry* did thank us publically in DC in front of all the plaintiffs for the idea of having all the plaintiffs meet in DC during the hearing. This is also the time when I came up with the idea of taking the 25' section #93 of the *Key West Rainbow 25 Sea-To-Sea flag* to DC. Section #93 was being cared for by *Fantasy Fest* king Stephen Sunday. With Steve Murray-Smith's permission, we brought that section of the flag with us to DC."

Susan remembers that she and Bernadette realized that a fundraiser would be necessary because even though the attorneys were working pro bono, there were other expenses involved in the time and effort to proceed with the project. Susan put together a fundraiser held at the *Bottle Cap.*

The group recalled receiving the endorsement of *HRC* – the *Human Rights Campaign* – at this time. As Susan reminds the group, their fund-raiser coincided with Key West Pride which is an annual June event, so it wasn't difficult to get participation, but it became clear that what should have been a local event that would allow locals to defray legal costs was turning into a fund-raising event for other entities. The group recalls thinking that it was very nice of *Equality Florida* to provide a cake for the event. They were rather surprised when they received a bill for $500 for that cake. Unsure what to do about it, they were counseled to ignore the bill. The event began to make obvious to them the fact that some groups used these events to make money for statewide initiatives and that there was a good amount of confusion among locals as to who actually benefitted from donations meant specifically for Aaron and Lee's lawyers.

Susan says, "It seems to me that *Equality Florida* had a way of celebrating whatever happened locally in Florida and then posting it to their website in a way that made it seem that they were somehow responsible for those local events. Their people wanted to get behind Aaron and Lee, cheering them on and saying 'Great job!' while posting photos that they did not have the rights to. Aaron and Lee never received any of the money that was donated specifically to support them." Aaron adds, "We got none. Bernadette's law firm got legal advice and $637 after we made multiple requests. We never would of asked for anything financially but Nadine Smith had offered this to us following our ruling."

Aaron agrees with Susan that things were happening so fast, control became a real challenge. Suddenly Judge David Audlin stepped down – see the chapter about his part in the case - and no one was sure who would replace him or who would hear the case or when a hearing would actually take place. Surprising everyone - including Aaron and Lee's attorney Bernadette Restivo - these things were decided swiftly. Bernadette was well-prepared and ready to deliver her case before Judge Luis Garcia who had been charged with redistributing all the cases previously assigned to Judge Audlin. He kept this one for himself. He issued his ruling in favor of Aaron and Lee on July 17, 2014, ten days after hearing Bernadette Restivo present her argument in favor of her plaintiffs.

Susan remembers that those days were marked by uncomfortable private conversations in which real information would be transmitted without giving the appearance of discord between the Huntsman/Jones team and the *Equality Florida* initiative. She says things were complicated by communication from *Equality Florida* saying they wanted to hold an event honoring Aaron and Lee. In March of 2015 *Equality Florida* bestowed on the couple its *Voice of Equality Award* at their annual Key West gala. Thankful for the honor but wary of being swallowed by an initiative that had not initially included them and did not have their best interests in mind, the team was hesitant to accept what *Equality Florida* offered.

MiKey has something to add to the picture at this point. He remembers that Susan was getting a lot of attention on Twitter about how their case was progressing. He developed a bladder infection that necessitated a trip to the emergency room assisted by his friend Mark Ebenhoch. That was when he formally introduced Mark to Aaron and Lee. The need for a central control for media had become obvious. Mark was exactly the right person for the job.

Mark remembers that Susan, Shannon and Bernadette were all very capable of providing parts of what the project required, but there needed to be some central direction. His first action was to forbid Aaron from discussing the details of his case on Facebook. Aaron jumped in at this point with a clarification, "I never discussed our case on Facebook. I only posted news articles and media reports. Mark was relieving the pressure we were under so we could get back to some kind of normalcy. Mark did have me create a new Facebook page called loveislovekw. Mark was more familiar with Twitter and he created

20

loveislovekw@twitter . I handed the new Facebook page over to him and showed him some insights. Mark tried to teach me about Twitter but I wasn't interested, having the new freedom of my own almost -normal Facebook page. Susan was also added to the new Facebook page as an administrator. loveislovekw@facebook eventually became Mark's personal page as he grew to love Facebook."

Mark convinced Aaron to channel all media inquiries to him. Aaron was happy to do this, having become unsure how to distinguish between good and bad requests. There was, for instance, what the team remembers as an offer of $500,000 from some sort of Satanist group that wanted their help attacking the governor of Florida. Aaron says, "They offered us $500,000 if they could back us. This is the same group that built a big statue in Oklahoma City and was on the front cover of many magazines."

Aaron remembers Bernadette calling him up with the question, "Who is this Mark guy?" Through Aaron, Mark told her to Google his name. As soon as Mark and Bernadette became acquainted, they became fast friends, and she never questioned his integrity and ability to work for the team. (You will learn more about them in their respective chapters of this book.)

What Mark remembers most about those days is the fact that Aaron and Lee were invited to march with a huge group including drag queens and *Equality Florida* in the annual Pride march. Mark says, "Everyone knows I have nothing against drag queens, but I didn't want our initiative swallowed up by such a large group. Aaron made some excuse about having a heart problem that made it impossible for him to march squeezed into that group, while I arranged to have us at the front of the march with all the political leaders. I called Bernadette and said, 'There's been a change of plan. Don't ask me what's going on, but meet us at the head of the march.' That is where we marched and it separated us from the circus."

Aaron describes that Pride march differently, saying, "I was still bitter about *Equality Florida* trying to charge our law firm for the meet-and-greet that Lee and I came up with - the $500 cake and finger sandwiches, and their asking for donations during the event. Mikey put them in their place, telling them to stop. I do have an existing heart issue and did call my doctor to have us moved away from the back of the parade to the front of the parade so we wouldn't be out in the heat of Pride for hours, sweating balls. And also, this meant that we wouldn't be surrounded by a Conch Republic wedding of two drag queens who aren't together anymore by the way. We felt it would make our fight for the freedom to marry look like a circus and not taken seriously before our court date. I didn't want to hurt anybody's feelings so I made the change and then told the law firm and others what I had done when we got to the staging site. I'm glad Mark came on the team a month later so I didn't have to worry about every detail of public appearance."

Mark and Susan say they swiftly learned to work as a team coordinating the fundraising efforts with Susan handling publicity and the actual event planning and with Mark handling all media inquiries. They were able to acquire an endorsement from the mayor's office at a time when he was up for re-election. Mark remembers writing to *Equality Florida* to introduce himself and to prohibit them from using photos of Aaron and Lee without his permission. He says it took a while for them to take him seriously and to honor the request.

The group does a fast-forward to a point in time after their victory in Monroe County and after the victory of the other plaintiffs in suits assisted by *Equality Florida* and other advocacy groups. That autumn was a time of tense jubilation as Florida saw Attorney General Pam Bondi's true colors in her needlessly aggressive appeal of the various rulings in favor of marriage equality and her unsuccessful attempts to have the judges' stays extended. (She did not drop her appeals until July 7, 2015.)

October meant the annual *Fantasy Fest*, Key West's biggest and wildest all-inclusive celebration that involves many parties, the crowning of a king and queen, and a dazzling parade down Duval Street. Aaron and Lee were invited to be the grand marshals of the parade but the invitation had to be kept a secret. Aaron says, "We knew for over two months that we were the grand marshals. This had to be kept a secret until the Coronation Ball on October 17, 2014." The idea was that the parade would be honoring and celebrating the string of Florida court victories that had overturned the homophobia of Anita Bryant and set the clocks ticking toward marriage equality in Florida. Key West's own bartender-heroes were at the pinnacle of those victories but until they arrived at the parade staging area they did not know that the pinnacle would be a literal one.

Mark says that the hardest thing he has ever done was to contain this secret. Their very small group knew about it, but even they had no idea that, as grand marshals, Aaron and Lee would be on a float at the top of a 30-foot high wedding cake, surrounded by dozens of couples on foot –

some of whom had decided not to file suit with Aaron and Lee but were now happy to celebrate their victory. They only knew that they had to be dressed in formal wedding attire and get to a certain place before the start of the parade. Susan remembers that the reason for the secrecy was the Fantasy Fest organizers' fear that there might be some protesters who would turn out to demonstrate against the very recent marriage equality rulings in Florida. They did not want to put Aaron and Lee in danger.

As the evening progresses, memories of events begin to overlap and blur. Aaron remembers being handed a script by *Equality Florida* with suggestions for good responses to media questions. He waved it away. He also remembers being amazed at how Lee blossomed during TV and radio interviews despite his shy nature and his very emotional sense of what they had accomplished as a couple. Susan remembers feeling that Aaron and Lee were the culmination of her earlier work on the *Sea-to-Sea Rainbow Flag* project, and that their marriage equality victory was for her a labor of love that she had never expected. Mark remembers the many opportunities for doing things a little differently if they had the chance to do it all again, but ultimately, their victory meant that everything unfolded perfectly. And MiKey? He just remembers telling them all over and over again, "We got this! We got this!" He was right.

GAY FLORIDA HISTORY

A Q&A With Fred Fejes

Even though Key West has its own unique gay history, it would be impossible to understand the victory of Aaron Huntsman and Lee Jones outside the context of gay Florida history. To place Huntsman and Jones correctly in the history of gay Florida, I spoke with Fred Fejes, PhD, the recognized authority about gay Florida history and culture, who teaches Media and Sexuality at Florida Atlantic University. My favorite among the books he has authored is *Gay Rights and Moral Panic: The Origins Of America's Debate On Homosexuality*. Currently he is director of the project "Generations: An Oral History of the South Florida Lesbian, Gay Bisexual and Transgender Community." I have read much of what Fred has written about gay Florida and I have written about Fred for *South Florida Gay News*, but I (perhaps self-indulgently) wanted a free-wheeling discussion with him. We met for brunch at The Floridian on Las Olas Boulevard in Fort Lauderdale where this Q&A was the result. My apologies to Fred for things I am misrepresenting, but on his Facebook page, he does state a fondness for gossip....

Anthony Adams: *Why and when did people begin to move to Florida? What was the attraction? Was there always a gay culture in Florida?*

Fred Fejes: Up until the late 1880s, people moved into northern Florida because that is as far as the railroads went. Just look at the maps of the 1860s and 1870s. All the railroads stopped in the first quarter of the top tier of the state. Up until the 1880s, people moved to Florida for agricultural work in cotton, rice and that kind of thing. It's only in the late 1880s and in the 1890s that Florida began to receive northerners with money who were not looking for farm work, the kind of people who, with post-Civil War and Industrial Revolution money, were looking for vacation spots. Harriet Beecher Stowe [Connecticut resident and author of *Uncle Tom's Cabin*] is an example. She wrote about how delighted she was to visit Florida in the winter because of the weather. Her words were typical of the publicity that was building about Florida as a destination. In 1876, there was a short story called *Felipe* by Constance Fenimore Wilson that is the first lesbian story to be published in America. It is about a young girl who is attracted to a woman tourist in Florida.

The development of Florida moved south with Flagler

[Henry Flagler, one of the founders of Standard Oil, built the railroad that connected Key West to mainland Florida.] as one of the major pioneers in terms of popularizing Florida as a tourist destination. He built a hotel in Saint Augustine but when he discovered that northern Florida could get a severe freeze, he expanded the railroad down to more temperate Palm Beach and Miami. Tourism was growing, but its development in Florida was uneven because the state really made its money from lumbering, farming and cattle. A visual example of early Florida tourism is the silent movie released in 1914 called "A Florida Enchantment" that told the story of a group of tourists at Flagler's Hotel Ponce de Leon in St. Augustine who eat magical seeds and are overcome with homosexual desires. To make the idea more palatable to viewers, at the end of the film, the whole adventure was revealed to have been just an odd dream. Tourism was a side development that took off only with the arrival of the automobile. In the 1920s, there was a big consumer boom with monied people starting to come down to Florida. That's when you could begin to differentiate between two groups: those who came down only for the winter and those who became permanent residents. There continued to be an influx of people from southern states who chose Florida not for the weather but for the opportunity to make money. In those years we had the beginning of a permanent south Florida-based population. Key West in many ways is a contradiction to everything I might say about historical Florida because it's older than the rest of Florida and it has its own history. It is almost like a Caribbean island rather than a part of Florida and it's hard to generalize about the people who moved there and the character of the population of Key West. The original Key West economy was based on fishing and the salvaging of wrecks. Much of its early population came from other islands such as Jamaica. Then came the tourism industry. Key West had its biggest boom after World War II with the development of airline transportation and the advent of air-conditioning and mosquito control that made it – and all of south Florida – livable year-round. So really, south Florida has a very recent population. On the other hand, if you go to north Florida, it's still very much like going to Georgia or Alabama, with an older more settled population that has been there for decades if not centuries.

AA: *Was there this sense that Florida was a place of sexual freedom – or that it could become such a place?*

FF: One of the things particular about south Florida is that it wasn't very settled, so there were no rules. If you moved there, you made up your own rules. If you look at a movie like "A Florida Enchantment" which was based on a stage play, you see that it explores the whole idea that Florida was a place where reality dissolves, things become different, and it captures the notion that Florida is a place where strange and exotic things happen. In the early part of the

20th century, the people who came down there had the sense that they could "let loose." In the 1920s, the liquor flowed in Miami and it was considered a place where you weren't watched. The level of political corruption was very high in Miami, but if you had money, you were fine.

AA: *In the early 20th century, Florida received James Deering who built the fabulous Vizcaya mansion in Miami, John Singer Sargent who was his frequent guest there, and Addison Mizner who gave south Florida a distinctive architectural look. Were they outliers or were they indicative of a growing gay culture in south Florida?*

FF: They were indicative of the kind of very diverse mix that you find there. I would not say they were indicative of a gay culture, not like New York or San Francisco. The main aspect of being gay in South Florida during those early decades was that it was better than being gay in say, Des Moines, for example. Things were so loose that as long as you didn't cause any problems or embarrass anybody, you got along fine and did very well. I think Mizner is a great example. Here he was in Palm Beach with no training as an architect, totally just winging it, and he creates this architectural style and feeds it to people who had money. It's strange and funny, but they looked at it and said, "Well that's pretty. Let's build it!" It was the type of environment in which you could invent yourself.

AA: *1930s Miami nightlife featured drag shows, but were they gay or were they just entertainment for straight tourists?*

FF: Those drag shows flourished in the 1940s but started in the 1930s. A bar called The Club Jewel Box had a famous drag revue. This was not geared to the gay audience. Drag performers weren't that offensive to most people in Miami in those years. In fact, I have seen memoirs and biographies of people who performed in drag and were carefully called female impersonators which was itself a long-standing tradition in performance and entertainment. The fact is many of them were gay but it wasn't gay entertainment. They kept their own personal sex lives private. If you were a female impersonator but made it obvious that you were homosexual, you risked getting kicked out of the drag show. The rule was "You can pretend, you can act, but don't really be it."

AA: *What changed in post-World War II Florida that made it become much more gay?*

FF: On the one hand, you have the early development of the gay rights movement in New York City. That movement got publicity, so there was a growing awareness of gay identity. In World War II, those who had served in the army where they met other gay soldiers or maybe had a gay experience far from home, realized that they were not doomed to be alone but that they were free to travel somewhere to find their tribe. Also at that time, Kinsey came out with his studies showing homosexuality as part of the natural scheme of things, so in terms of the larger culture there was this awareness among gay people everywhere that they were a lot more common than had been presumed before World War II.

AA: *Are you saying that a gay soldier who came home to Des Moines after his discharge would find his hometown restrictive and maybe remember having had a great gay week in Miami and decide to move there?*

FF: Right. That would be an impetus. Also, you had wealthy gay men coming down here where their money went much further and afforded them a luxurious lifestyle. There was an energetic cross-pollination between wealthy gay men and the young gay men who moved or visited here and were guests at their parties. I interviewed a man whose family owned Dalton Locomotive Works. He lived in Coconut Grove in the 1970s. He told me that many wealthy gay men had parties on their yachts in Biscayne Bay. They would line up their yachts and have these progressive dinners in which you'd have drinks at one, appetizers at another, and go from one yacht to the next through dessert. Young men prized invitations to these parties. Coconut Grove became the center of gay life in Miami.

AA: *In the 1950s, was there some kind of odd tolerance of gay nightlife in south Florida that didn't match what was going on elsewhere in the country?*

FF: I would say there was some tolerance, but I wouldn't say that what was happening in Florida was exceptional. It just expressed itself differently. At that time, Miami had no laws against cross-dressing. New York did have laws against it. So, you had a huge drag scene down there that you wouldn't find in other places, and a lot of these drag performers were from the Northeast. They came down here to perform without problems. In 1965, however, the city passed a series of laws in reaction to the rumors that gay men were victimizing children. This hysteria almost killed the whole drag scene.

AA: *You have written about "moral panic" and how it scapegoats the gay community. How and when did that happen in Florida? How successful was it in Miami? How successful was the Johns Committee in Gainesville? The raid on the Club Miami? The crackdown on the "Friends of Emma Jones?" event?*

FF: The Johns Committee was a very successful witch hunt on the part of politicians in the early '60s against homosexuals in state universities. They tried to expand their persecution into other Florida schools, but in south Florida they were not successful because schools were more locally controlled and also because the *Miami Herald* was a really strong opponent of the Johns Committee. That paper fought to make sure that south Florida was off-limits to the Johns Committee. There were many moments in south Florida gay history when that newspaper was very helpful in protecting gay rights. Of course, if you were a gay teacher or student in South Florida, you were aware of the Johns Committee and you had to be careful about your actions. The witch hunt succeeded in Gainesville but failed in south Florida because they got bold with their success. In Gainesville their persecution was under the radar of most people, but in south Florida, they circulated hostile anti-gay pamphlets. People became aware of what the Johns Committee was really all about, there was an outcry against it and the committee was disbanded.

You asked about the raid on the Club Miami which was a bathhouse. That happened in 1976. Jack Campbell was its owner. He had moved to Miami in the late 1960s. He was a really sweet guy and he was a good businessman. He had some early involvement with the Mattachine Society. [An early gay rights organization] He came down to Miami knowing how to make business deals. He hired a lawyer and researched the laws that might apply to bathhouses. He created a private club because of the laws protecting those organizations. Jack's big asset was that he was not ashamed of being openly and proudly gay around other business people. To make a lot of money at his business, he decided to expand nationally, going to an area like Indiana where he met with local business people who are more interested in money than morals. He would share his successful business plan with investors and promise them that there'd be a draw on a huge closeted gay community. He promised to make his clubs friendly, clean and safe. He stayed out of big cities like Chicago and he ended up doing very well that way and by the end of the 1970s, the Club Bath chain was really one of the first national chains or organizations of that could be described as gay. It was so well established nationally that if you wanted to get a message to the gay community you would advertise at those bathhouses. In 1976, the city of Miami decided they were going to make a show of their moral superiority by raiding the Club Baths. However, the fact that Campbell had money and lived in Coconut Grove reflected the kind of diverse place that Miami was, and would make him a formidable opponent. The Miami Herald treated him respectfully in its approach to the story. Basically, the bathhouse was an easy target for a sheriff who wanted to make it seem as if he was doing his job well. Campbell ultimately won his defense against the raid and even ran for public office.

You also asked about "The Friends Of Emma Jones." In the late 1960s, a small group of gay friends in Pensacola started an annual beach party that swiftly grew to include a few thousand participants who came from all parts of Florida and nearby southern states. It became a weeklong event. It got so big that by the early 1970s, the local police had to shut it down, but that party provided the inspiration for many Florida gay groups and campus organizations that finally saw a way to network and socialize and to be strong in demanding rights. Today, we take for granted circuit parties like Miami's White Party or Winter Party, but the "Friends of Emma Jones" party was a real innovation.

AA: *In the 60s and 70s there was a rise in gay activism and gay identity in south Florida. Did it keep pace with what was happening in the rest of the country? Were we ahead or behind? In those decades, was Key West unique in south Florida? Was it an oasis of gay freedom or is that just an illusion?*

FF: It would be really difficult to measure that comparison between Florida activism and what was happening elsewhere. Let's look at what we did have in south Florida in those years. There was the establishment of the MCC Church in Miami in the late 1960s. The earliest Gay Pride celebrations date to the early 1970s. In that same decade, you had the formation of gay groups to coincide with political conventions that took place in Miami. South

Florida was never a cauldron of gay activism, because, as you know, down here, politics and activism not tops on the list of reasons why people move here. Also, there weren't a lot of big universities with a critical mass of engaged students who were going to go out and be gay activists.

AA: *Did the influx of people from Cuba and Puerto Rico have an influence on gay culture in south Florida? Positive or negative?*

FF: Yes, but initially it was negative because immigrant Cubans were anti-gay. In their view, being gay meant you were not masculine or macho. As things progress into first, second and third generation American-born Cubans, things became very positive. You could compare it to other immigrant experiences, like the Italian immigration in New York. Both groups were not recreating their culture over successive generations. In Miami, the immigrant groups made a family-based culture very strong. This gave the city stability both culturally and socially. The earliest Latino/Cuban gay groups that tried to protest Anita Bryant in Miami were not successful because of the strong family traditions they were up against.

AA: *In the 80s, how did AIDS impact the growth of the visible gay community in south Florida?*

FF: I moved here in 1986 and even though AIDS appeared in 1983, it was only in the mid 1980s that it became really visible and at first it was considered just something that men who cruised gay bars got. But then other people were getting sick. The point is that it was easy to dismiss at first because the first wave of victims were doing things that most gay men supposedly would never do. As in other urban communities, gay men in south Florida thought that only the most promiscuous would get it. You would say to yourself, "If I have sex with only three men in a bathhouse instead of ten men, I'm safe." Like everywhere, it was difficult to get the gay community to respond and to create concern in the larger community. It was only when prominent men started coming down with AIDS that this changed. I remember reading the obituaries and searching for the ones about young single men. The obituaries rarely identified what they died of. Every so often you would find one saying that the deceased had a "longtime companion." This was such a powerful phrase because we were so hungry to see the truth. And then of course there were national campaigns against AIDS, and people down here saw what was being done elsewhere and followed suit. I think one characteristic that I noticed down here in south Florida had to do with it being a place of wealth. There were these huge glittery AIDS benefit balls and events in which you very rarely saw the word "gay" or "sex." It was as if the entire AIDS campaign had to be scrubbed if it was going to work. And I said to myself, "Well okay, this is what you have to do to get the money." But it was galling to see it. I think also down here at that time there was an attempt to create a kind of ACT-UP movement. [AIDS Coalition To Unleash Power] it didn't go very far. It didn't tap well into the political energy of South Florida.

AA: *Did LGBT activism in the 90s pave the way for the permanent establishment of the gay culture of south Florida that exists today?*

FF: Yes. What people did in the 1980s and 1990s really laid the groundwork, so that after the 2003 Supreme Court case [Lawrence v. Texas, striking down state sodomy laws] people started coming out, and the new gay visibility made the gay community trendy and powerful.

AA: *If you had to list three or four historical facts about gay south Florida that brought about marriage equality in Florida, what would they be?*

FF: I think the most important event was the 1977 Anita Bryant situation because it really showed for the first time the size and scope of the gay and lesbian community in south Florida. For the first time, our community was present, alive, active and showing its face. The second thing was the AIDS crisis and the kind of community organizing and publicity it gave to the gay community, It also gave the community a face and moved us beyond sex and into concern for human lives in a very real way. A third factor was the media publicity in the 1960s. The newspapers stopped portraying gay men as sex maniacs. Now they were appearing in the media as real people with a normalcy about them. It's a different narrative that the media in south Florida began to use, and of course that led to the point where people could accept the notion that gay marriage was okay. And finally, we have to acknowledge the importance of gay adoption, and the new public awareness that there is such a thing as lesbian and gay families. The adoption debate was lengthy in Florida. It didn't seem to make much national news, but there were a number of cases that made it clear that there were lesbian and gay families pushing for adoption rights. I have to say I was very surprised at the sudden progress we had on gay marriage here in Florida. It seemed that gay advocacy organizations had been saying, "Let's solve our other problems and get our other rights first. Then we can look at gay marriage." In some ways, you know, these guys [Huntsman and Jones] jumped things and got marriage done and accelerated the discussion. It's just so great that they did that, and I was happy to see that happen.

A BRIEF AND ANECDOTAL HISTORY OF GAY KEY WEST

To construct a suitable history of gay Key West is to smile and laugh at the memory of folks who washed up onto its shores without washing out, and without fear of strong colors, stronger words or strongest drink. To understand the mindset of gay Key West is to set aside the presumptive grid of cultural segregations that govern the growth of most other communities. To understand the gay people of Key West, you must also understand the straight people of Key West because the two groups are so intricately and pleasantly knit, you can't see one without the other. As a prelude to understanding the history of gay Key West, read William Golding's novel *Lord Of The Flies* in which a band of lost boys revert to wild but primal behavior when left to fend for themselves on an uninhabited island. Gay Key West is similar, but with more frequent and enduring happy endings.

Perhaps the speediest route to acquiring an anecdotal history of gay Key West is to read Hanns Ebensten's 2004 book *Home and Abroad* containing the delightful chapter *At Home in Key West* about the years he spent there as an older man with his "friend" Brian. (He preferred the genteel old-school terminology rather than the more modern "partner/lover/husband.") Ebensten is considered the "father of gay travel" having invented the industry in 1972. The company he founded, now called **HE**travel – honoring his initials - and headquartered in Key West, is still the worldwide leader in the gay adventure and cultural tour business. Ebensten had been in the travel business for 22 years when he founded his company because, having been on a rafting expedition in the Grand Canyon in the unfortunate company of fussy and annoying traveling companions, he knew that assembling a group of like-minded gay men would make the experience more satisfying. He was right about that, and HEtravel's president Phil Sheldon has built upon the Ebensten tradition, continuing to offer the best tours of the best places on earth. HEtravel is for LGBT people who like traveling with like-minded folks.

Ebensten moved to Key West in 1977, buying a house on quaint Peacon Lane – originally called Grunt Bone Alley -- in Key West's "Old Town."

I first heard about Key West in 1962, when the perceptive British author, James Morris, wrote of it that "everywhere men are lazing about with no shirts on. It is a little city dedicated to easy living. At night, along Duval Street, a colorful crowd saunters and sips and gossips. In little cafés you can while away the hours listening to music and eating pungent Cuban sandwiches. Patio restaurants, in the courtyards of old houses, offer immensely long and varied meals. You can sip good wines and talk to artists, profane seamen, idlers, scientists and collectors of shells."

Not much has changed.

Our nextdoor neighbor was – and still is – Walt Desel, a versatile painter who had been a major in the US Marine Corps. His house bears a hand-lettered sign PEOPLE ON PEACON LANE DO NOT COMPLAIN and was the smallest gay guesthouse on Key West, advertised as "Where your fantasies come true."

Desel, a snowbird who summered on Fire Island, was typical of the creative spirit of those who fell in love with Key West and had to become a part of it.

Lest we get too idyllic a picture of Ebensten's Key West, he goes on to say,

The only detriment to our otherwise contented existence was the nasty little monster who lived at the corner of Peacon Lane and Caroline Street and sold popcorn on Mallory Square at

sunset. He was violently homophobic and put up signs on his house saying: MAKE KEY WEST FAG FREE and STOP AIDS KILL FAGS. The latter sign had a picture of one stickman sodomizing another and was particularly offensive because three men living on the lane at that time were dying of AIDS.

I complained about the signs to the authorities at City Hall and they ordered them to be removed, which incensed the popcorn man even more. When Brian and I walked out of our lane into Caroline Street and he saw us, he shouted, " Walk out of the lane by the other end. I don't want to see you fags outside my house!" And he tried to run us down with his motorscooter and called out, "Out of my way, girls!"

Ebensten notes that the popcorn man ran for mayor but received only forty votes. He also notes that a man who did win a Key West mayoral race circulated campaign posters saying, "ALL YOU NEED IN LIFE IS TREMENDOUS SEX DRIVE AND A GREAT EGO – BRAINS DON'T MEAN A SHIT." Given the banter in the 2016 presidential campaign, Key West does not seem so extraordinary in its politics.

Ebensten's knowledge of Key West history went well beyond squabbles with neighbors on Peacon Lane.

*In 1819, Spain ceded Florida to the United States. In 1820,
Commodore David Porter established a naval base in Key
West to suppress piracy. He was greatly impressed with the
island's location as a military and naval station and said of it
that it had no equal except Gibraltar. Shipwrecks occurred
daily on the treacherous reefs along the Florida Keys and
wrecking was the chief occupation and made many early
settlers rich. Experienced sponge divers came from the
Bahamas and cigar makers from Cuba.*

*In 1912, Henry Flagler built the railroad that linked Key
West to the mainland. By the 1920s, the Casa Marina, the
La Concha and more than a dozen smaller hotels and inns
provided 600 rooms for tourists, but the great hurricane of
1935 swept away the railroad and put an end to tourism. The
sponging industry was ruined by disease. Only the navy
continued to play a major role and sustain the city's economy
until after World War II, when tourism revived and
prosperity returned.*

*Members of families that first came to Key West in the 1820s
– the Currys, Geigers, Porters, Roberts, Ottos – are as proud
of their heritage as those in England whose ancestors arrived
there with William the Conqueror in 1066 A.D. The symbol
of Key West is the conch shell, and residents who are born
there proudly refer to themselves as Conchs. The old wooden*

houses, raised on stilts off the ground to survive hurricanes and with pretty frilly trim, are Conch Houses. Old cars, their sides often gaudily painted with representations of flowers, birds and fish, and so dilapidated as to be beyond repair yet still able to drag themselves wheezing along the streets, are Conch Cruisers. Bicycles in such ruinous condition that no one ever thinks of stealing them, are Conch Bikes.

The Conch families rule Key West, as they should, and although I feel more at home there than I have felt anywhere in my long life, I fully appreciate that I am and always will be an outsider.

In 1979, the Reverend Morris Wright of the Key West Baptist Temple launched a campaign to rid Key West of newcomers, in particular of homosexuals, and paid for advertisements in the local newspaper in which he announced:

> *"If I were the chief of police I would get me a hundred good men, give them each a baseball bat and have them walk down Duval Street and dare one of those freaks to stick his head over the edge of the sidewalk. You could easily get a hundred good men to serve in that capacity for a few hours. I know at least five hundred who would be only too happy to serve."*

He went on to say that female impersonators and queers should be loaded into a deputy's automobile and shipped to the county line and told to get going back where such belonged. "Half of Duval Street is filled with disgusting, immoral, practically naked excuses for human beings. Say it can't be done? Yes it can. All we need is some good old fashioned guts and morals."

A number of pious Baptist youths formed themselves into gangs, armed themselves with baseball bats and clubs, and followed patrons of the gay bars and discotheque on Duval Street at night through the dark streets and attacked and injured them there. When these incidents became frequent, the owners of inns with a gay clientele organized unarmed patrols to escort their guests back to their lodgings. Tennessee Williams, Key West's most illustrious citizen, walking on Duval Street at night with his friend Dotson Rader, was beaten up but chose not to lodge a complaint, having been informed that among his attackers were the sons of several local police officers and firemen. "I like living here, and I want to continue to do so," he said.

The ensuing national – indeed international – press publicity was not beneficial to Key West tourism and the Tourist Development Association asked the Reverend Morris Wright to order his gangs to discontinue their persecution of tourists, who were spending much needed money in the city.

By no means did all Key West citizens approve of the good Baptist and the tactics by which he wanted to rid the town of "queers." Gay men, both residents and visitors, were overwhelmingly accepted and welcomed, providing that they behaved decently and with propriety. The gay men had learnt a bitter lesson and did not continue to behave in Key West as if it was their town. They were and still are, only a small minority and they no longer flaunted themselves so blatantly in public in what is a small and conservative town where families with children predominate.

Ebensten gives us glimpses into the eccentric lives and ventures of the folks of Key West, giving the impression that if he had chosen to live on a different street, he would have soon acquired hundreds of different but equally fascinating stories.

The warm languid air of Key West is conducive to persons who hatch impractical and unrealistic schemes. There is the man who visited Cuba, became enamoured of young Cuban men, returned to Key West and collected money and medical and food supplies for Cuba, all of which would have been put to better use if he had donated them to the local branch of the Salvation Army. He shuttled for many years between Key West and Cuba and made efforts for them to be declared Sister Islands – but to make siblings of a little island four miles long with thirty-thousand people, and the island nation of Cuba, 2,500 miles long and with a population of more than ten million was like proposing to mate a flee with an elephant.

Then there were the enthusiastic Key Westers who, in 1982, wanted the island to secede from the United States and become an autonomous Conch Republic, cheerfully ignoring the fact that the island is dependent on the mainland for its supplies of water and power and food. The mayor announced that he was now the first prime minister of the new republic; other ministerial posts and those of ambassadors in foreign countries were offered to the highest bidders. But what began in seriousness soon became a joke, with Conch Republic Days boisterously celebrated each year, and tourists avidly buying Conch Republic flags, T-shirts, car license plates and passports.

Ebensten is full of tales about dinners at the homes of gay male couples and ménages-a-trois "who like to cook – and do it well – and where the dinner tables by the pool are set with Meissen or Limoges china and there is always stimulating conversation and often bawdy gossip." He encounters a hustler whose "office" was the local launderette, and dubious doctors fond of drugs, and visiting pro football players open to new games. Ebensten never lacked for diversion.

Until I moved to Key West, I had always lived in large cities with endless attractions, and my friends thought that I would be bored in a small town.

But life in Key West is never dull and continues to provide me with surprises.

My greatest daily pleasure is to swim at 7:30 in the morning three or four times round the raft that is moored fifty feet off the Pier House Hotel beach in the Gulf of Mexico, and then walk back home for breakfast. The raft was a scene of an event that has become a Key West legend. Two carefree young men, high on drink and drugs and totally oblivious of their surroundings, were making love on it one afternoon in full view of the people on the beach and the terrace of the restaurant. The hotel management ordered one of the beach attendants to swim out and tell them to stop their activities immediately. "But why? No one can see us here!" they cried.

When Ebensten turned 80, he befriended an enchanting young Radical Faerie named Brad who owned nothing but a pair of frayed shorts.

In 1977, when my dear Brian and I bought out house in Key West, Brian planted a very small cutting from an Australian tree in front of the house, which he had brought back (illegally) from the Cape York Peninsula in Northern Queensland, where it is known by the natives as Raki Tali, "the red tree," due to its vivid red blossoms; its botanical name is "bracialiptus." Twenty-five years later it was more than forty feet tall and one of its branches was interfering with the telephone lines. I could not reach it by using my stepladder, and since Brad says that there is no tree that he cannot climb, I asked him if he could cut off the branch. "Sure," he said, "but if so, I'll do it naked."

The tree is directly on the lane, but as there is almost no traffic and very few people walk there, I agreed. "But please be quick," I said.

He stripped off his shorts and climbed up as nimble as a monkey. At that moment, a tourist came walking down the lane, intending to photograph the typical old Conch houses. He saw Brad in the tree and asked to take a picture; permission was granted, and then I was dismayed because a policeman appeared, to pay a social call on one of the tenants in the house opposite, but he merely gave the naked man in the tree a glance of complete indifference.

That's Key West.

I spoke with Dennis Beaver, president of the Board of Directors of the "Tennessee Williams Key West Exhibit" located at 513 Truman Avenue, to gain another perspective on the history of gay Key West. His organization honors Williams, a Key West icon who visited and lived in Key West from 1941 until his death in 1983. Beaver says, "The mission of the Tennessee Williams Key West Exhibit is to collect, preserve, and showcase historic archival materials directly related to the writings and artistic creations that won Tennessee Williams multiple awards."

He echoes much of what Ebensten says about the evolution of the gay community in Key West and its assimilation and successful overcoming of moments of adversity.

Beaver says, "Our annual Fantasy Fest is a great example. It was started in 1979 by a group of gay business owners who wanted an event to attract visitors during the rather slow month of October. At first it was a gay Mardi Gras sort of thing, but as the years went by, it became more non-gay, mainly because all the businesses wanted to participate. Most of its attendees are from south Florida. Now it's a huge and fully inclusive celebration.

"Gay Key Westers were certainly responsible for the rehabilitation of the historic district. Tennessee Williams who moved to Key West permanently in 1949 himself said that there were more and more homosexuals doing more and more renovations. He, of course, put Key West on the literary map because once he moved here, people from New York -- all the famous writers and theater people -- visited him. He had so many famous actors and actresses down here. He hosted Gore Vidal, Truman Capote, Tallulah Bankhead and so many others."

In large measure, the gay community of Key West was the most powerful economic driver in the second half of the last century, but only gradually an accepted part of its life. Beaver moved to Key West from New York in 1979. He says, "In the early 50s, it was not safe to walk down the street and be obviously gay. It was very much a navy town. When the navy decreased it presence, things changed. Of course, gays have always been on the forefront of cultural growth. These days, it doesn't much matter what your sexuality is. That was our goal decades ago. We have almost made it. We are not quite there yet, but almost.

"The two major happenings helped bring about gay inclusion in Key West. The first was in the mid-1980s when the religious right took over the Christmas parade and they refused to allow any gay float in the parade. There was a huge uproar about this. Many people who found out about the exclusion of the gay groups dropped out of the parade. Others stayed in, but just to protest along the route. Even some well established churches were not in favor of this. The MCC float that had been denied entry was invited by the Catholic Church to be parked right in front of their church. The Gay Business Guild protested the exclusion for many months. As a result, the city took over the parade and made sure that it reverted to being all-inclusive.

"There was a similar effort to get the gay out of Fantasy Fest but the city put a stop to that immediately. I think these two fights did not set us back but moved us forward, and only served to make the gay community of Key West stronger. One of the most interesting Fantasy Fests I remember was when an all-naturist/nudist cruise was in port at the time. That only added to the mix!"

Beaver says that people always wonder if Key West is still as gay as it had once been. Out-of-town gays sometimes ask that question when considering a visit. He says, "People are always talking about the fact that there are fewer gay guesthouses in Key West. That may be true, but that doesn't mean that Key West is any less gay. There are over 60 guesthouses in town. Now, you can come to Key West with your straight friends and family members and stay together almost anywhere because most of them are inclusive. This actually serves to strengthen gay tourism.

"We have become deeply accustomed to our casual life of inclusion. We are not clannish. Even if we have a benefit event for a gay cause, 75% of the attendance might be straight."

The motto of Key West is "One Human Family." They happily practice what they preach.

LARRY BLACKBURN PHOTOGRAPHY

A FLORIDA MARRIAGE EQUALITY TIMELINE

January 18, 1977 – Ruth Shack, Metro-Dade County Commissioner, successfully sponsors an amendment to the existing anti-discrimination ordinance of the county, adding a ban on discrimination based on sexual orientation. Among the most vocal protestors is pop singer, beauty pageant queen and spokeswoman for the Florida Citrus Commission Anita Bryant, whose talent agent is married to Ruth Shack. Bryant had contributed to Shack's election campaign. Bryant said she feared for the safety of her children should homosexuals be allowed to be teachers.

June 17, 1977 – Bryant, founder and president of *Save Our Children*, an organization that spread homophobia in the county and collected signatures to force a referendum on the anti-discrimination ordinance, succeeds in her efforts to repeal it by a margin of 69 to 31 percent. Her win spawns similar victories in Fort Lauderdale, Gainesville, Palm Beach and in other states, but also serves to strengthen and mobilize the gay community in Florida and throughout the country.

1977 - Florida officially bans same-sex marriage and gay adoption. The adoption prohibition would be reversed 31 years later when Miami-Dade Circuit Court Judge Cindy S. Lederman declared it unconstitutional on November 25, 2008.

1997 - the Florida Legislature enacts a law restricting marriage to the "union between one man and one woman." The law also prohibits Florida from recognizing same-sex marriages performed in other states.

1998 - Miami-Dade County vanquishes Anita Bryant's *Save Our Children* campaign, reauthorizing an anti-discrimination ordinance banning discrimination based on sexual orientation.

December 4, 2001 - In the appeal of the earlier dismissal of the lawsuit, the Fifth District Court of Appeals rules in *Frandsen v. County of Brevard* that someone's "sex" is not basic to the state constitution's equality protections. The suit was primarily focused on the prohibition of public exposure of female breasts when men breasts may be exposed. Its failure included the rationale that a different decision would have allowed for same-sex marriage in Florida.

2002 - a Miami-Dade County ballot initiative that sought to repeal the 1998 equal rights law is voted down by 56 percent of the voters.

June 15, 2003 – To celebrate the 25th anniversary of the creation of his flag, Gilbert Baker makes a 1.4 miles long eight-color gay flag that is stretched the length of Duval Street connecting the Atlantic Ocean to the Gulf Coast Sea. Aaron Huntsman is brought in from Fort Lauderdale by Absolut Vodka to work on this project. That is when he meets Lee

Jones. He also meets Susan Kent who, as the president of Key West Gay And Lesbian Community Center, is coordinating the project.

2004 – The same-sex weddings in San Francisco spark a number of local demands for marriage equality in Florida communities. The Florida activism was geared to raising awareness of the issue.

February 25, 2004 - Attorney Ellis Ruben files a suit against Broward County Clerk Howard Forman on behalf of a couple, James Stewart and Wayne Ellis Clark, and 170 gays and lesbians demanding marriage equality. Forman was personally in favor of marriage equality but could not issue licenses to same-sex couples because of Florida laws.

March 16, 2004 - Key West initiates a "White Ribbon" campaign for marriage equality at a meeting of the City Commission.

March 19, 2004 – Eight same-sex couples go to Orlando City Hall, requesting marriage licenses. They are turned away.

March 22, 2004 – Same-sex couples gather in Gainesville at the Alachua County Courthouse requesting marriage licenses. They are turned away.

April 15, 2004 – On tax day, six Monroe County couples file a suit in Key West because they were denied marriage licenses. They are Joan Higgs and Sandra Carlile; Charles W. Martin and Timothy Bryan Carpenter; Javier Reynalos and Tim Sheehan; William Hazelton and Gary Gethen; Jane Mannix-Lachner and Victoria Barber; and Steven Robinson and Rev. Geoff Leonard. *Equality Florida* is also a plaintiff in the suit.

November 4, 2008 - voters approve "Amendment 2" which adds Section 27 to Article 1 of the Florida state constitution: "Marriage defined: Inasmuch as marriage is the legal union of only one man and one woman as husband and wife, no other legal union that is treated as marriage or the substantial equivalent thereof shall be valid or recognized." A minimum of 60% of voters was required for the passage of the initiative. It received 62%. Governor Charlie Crist supports the amendment. In Monroe County, less than 50% of voters support the amendment.

March 24, 2009 – Gainesville voters defeat a referendum that would have removed LGBT protections.

2013 - *Equality Florida* and *Freedom to Marry* launch a joint initiative "Get Engaged" to overturn "Amendment 2" which had banned same-sex marriage in Florida in 2008.

June 26, 2013 – The US Supreme Court rules on *United States v. Windsor*, declaring Section 3 of DOMA (The Defense of Marriage Act) that defined marriage as exclusively the union of one man and one woman to be unconstitutional.

September 23, 2013 – Attorney Nancy Brodzki files *Brassner v. Lade* in Broward. Heather Brassner seeks a divorce from her same-sex partner with whom she was joined in a civil union in Vermont in 2002. According to Attorney Brodzki, this is the first marriage case filed after the Windsor decision.

2014 – polling in Florida beings to show a steady reversal in support for same-sex marriage with a majority of Florida residents in favor of marriage equality.

January 15, 2014 – In *Shaw v. Shaw*, Keiba Lynn and Mariama Shaw, who had been married in Massachusetts and were living in Florida, file a petition for divorce in Hillsborough County. Their case is rejected and their attempts to appeal are unsuccessful.

January 21, 2014 – *Pareto v. Ruvin*: six Florida couples (Catherina Pareto and Karla Arguello; Dr.

Juan Carlos Rodriguez and David Price; Vanessa and Melanie Alenier; Todd and Jeff Delmay; Summer Greene and Pamela Faerber; and Don Price Johnston and Jorge Isaias Diaz) with Equality Florida and the National Center for Lesbian Rights (NCLR) file a lawsuit in Miami against Florida's same-sex marriage ban.

March 6, 2014 – *Brenner v. Scott* suit is filed in which one same-sex couple seeks recognition of their out-of-state marriage. A second same-sex couple seeking marriage in Florida is added to this suit.

March 13, 2014 – Florida ACLU files *Grimsley and Albu v. Scott* suit for SAVE representing eight couples asking for recognition of their out-of-state marriages.

April 1, 2014 – Aaron Huntsman and Lee Jones apply for a marriage license at the office of the Monroe County Clerk, and are denied that license. Attorney Bernadette Restivo files their lawsuit In Monroe County.

April 30, 2014 – Arlene Goldberg's request to be named as wife on her recently deceased spouse's death certificate is added to the ACLU's *Grimsley and Albu v. Scott* suit.

May 14, 2014 – *Dousset v. Florida Atlantic University*: Glidas Dousset, a student at FAU, wishes to have his 2013 Massachusetts marriage to Florida resident Paul Rubio recognized in order to qualify for the in-state tuition rate granted to the spouses of Florida residents.

July 1 2014 - Judge Sarah Zabel of the 11th Circuit Court hears oral arguments in the case of the six couples with Equality Florida.

July 7, 2014 – Monroe County Circuit Judge Luis Garcia hears oral arguments in the case of Huntsman v. Heavilin (Aaron Huntsman and Lee Jones) the law firm Restivo & Vigil-Fariñas represents the couple.

July 17, 2014 - Judge Garcia rules in favor of Aaron Huntsman and Lee Jones, striking down Florida's ban on same-sex marriage and ordering Monroe County to issue them a marriage license. The decision is stayed to allow for appeal by Florida Attorney General Pam Bondi.

July 25, 2014 - Judge Zabel in Miami rules against Florida's ban on same-sex marriage. The decision is stayed to allow for appeal by Florida Attorney General Pam Bondi.

August 4, 2014 - Broward Circuit Court Judge Dale Cohen issues a ruling in favor of Heather Brassner who sought a divorce from her wife, becoming the third judge to strike down Florida's ban on same-sex marriage. Judge Cohen vacates the decision explaining that the state must be given enough time to file an appeal. (See **Dec 8, 2014** for his reversal.)

August 5, 2014 - Circuit Judge Diane Lewis rules in

favor of William Simpson who had married Francis C. Bangor in Delaware in 2013. Bangor owned a home In Boynton Beach, Florida at the time of his death on March 15, 2014. Bangor had named Simpson as his executor, but Florida law requires a non-resident executor ("personal representative") to be a relative. Judge Lewis ruled that this law was unconstitutional and that Simpson should be recognized as the surviving spouse. Because the Florida Attorney General was not a part of the case, Judge Lewis did not stay her order, issuing letters of administration to Simpson, making him the executor of Bangor's estate, and also making their marriage the first same-sex marriage to be recognized in Florida.

August 21, 2014 - Federal Judge Hinkle rules that Florida's ban on marriage is unconstitutional in the federal cases *Brenner v. Scott* and *Grimsley v. Scott.* Judge Hinkle puts a stay in place to expire on January 5th, 2015. (Not subject to the stay is Hinkle's decision in favor of Arlene Goldberg who had petitioned the court to revise the death certificate of her deceased wife Carol Goldwasser. Goldberg and Goldwasser had married in 2011 in

New York.)

August 28, 2014 – The Third District Court of Appeals in Miami denies Attorney Pam Bondi's request to have Judges Zabel and Garcia's rulings set aside until the US Supreme Court rules on marriage equality.

October 24, 2014 - *Brandon-Thomas v. Brandon-Thomas* : Danielle Brandon-Thomas and Krista Brandon-Thomas were married in Massachusetts in October, 2012. The couple moved to Florida where Danielle filed for divorce in October of 2013 with Krista contesting the action because their marriage was not recognized by Florida. The court dismissed the petition for divorce.

November 5, 2014 - Judge Hinkle rejects a request that his stay be lifted.

December 1, 2014 – *Wall-DeSousa v. Florida DMV*: a same-sex couple who had combined their last names with a hyphen when they were married in New York in 2013, is ordered by the DMV to have their Florida licenses show their pre-marriage names.

December 3, 2014 - an Eleventh Circuit panel denies Attorney General Pam Bondi's request that Judge Hinkle's stay be extended.

December 8, 2014 - Judge Cohen again rules in favor of granting Heather Brassner a divorce. He does not issue a stay because Attorney General Pam Bondi and the state of Florida are not listed as defendants. On December 17, 2014, Judge Cohen grants Heather Brassner a divorce.

December 19, 2014 - The United States Supreme Court denies a request to extend the stay on marriage equality in Florida.

January 1, 2015 - United States District Judge Robert L. Hinkle clarifies his marriage ruling, affirming that *all* Florida counties must issue marriage licenses to same-sex couples after the expiration of the stay on January 5, 2015.

January 2, 2015 - William Lee Jones and Aaron Huntsman, go to the Monroe County Clerk's Office where they complete a marriage license application.

January 5, 2015: Judge Sable lifts the stay on her marriage ruling, allowing marriages to begin in Miami-Dade County on January 5, 2015 in the afternoon.

Jan 5, 2015 - The Monroe County Clerk of Courts' office closes at 5 p.m., but reopens at 11:30 p.m. to allow same-sex couples to fill out applications for marriage licenses.

Jan 6, 2015 - At 12:01 AM, Aaron Huntsman and Lee Jones receive their license, and are married on the steps of the Monroe County Courthouse.

April 24, 2015 – The Second District Court of Appeals in Florida reverses the decision that had denied Danielle Brandon-Thomas her divorce in - *Brandon-Thomas v. Brandon-Thomas* . (See **October 24, 2014**)

April 2015 – Dan Bready and Kevin Dickinson host the Key West contingent at their home in Washington, DC, where they host a rooftop reception for the plaintiffs in town for the Supreme Court hearing.

April 27, 2015 – Aaron Huntsman and Lee Jones greet marriage equality plaintiffs in 55 cases in 33 states and spanning 40 years at a DC reception they conceived with Mark Ebenhoch and Louisiana plaintiff Derek Penton-Robicheaux, and hosted by *Freedom to Marry* on the eve of the Supreme Court hearing of *Obergefell v. Hodges*. The White House's Valerie Jarrett, Senior Advisor to the President of the U.S., toasted the group.

April 28, 2015 - The U.S. Supreme Court hears oral arguments on the marriage equality case *Obergefell v. Hodges.*

June 26, 2015 - In a 5-4 decision, with an opinion by Justice Kennedy, the U.S. Supreme Court rules in favor of the plaintiffs in *Obergefell v. Hodges* (a consolidation of several marriage cases) making freedom to marry for same-sex couples legal in all 50 states. Marriage equality becomes the law of the land.

July 7, 2015 – Florida Attorney General Pam Bondi drops her appeal of the rulings in both the Miami-Dade and Monroe Counties same-sex marriage cases.

July 17, 2015 – William Lee Jones and Aaron Huntsman celebrate their wedding in Key West at the Ernest Hemingway House.

AARON HUNTSMAN

Aaron Huntsman had no idea what he wanted but he knew he had to keep moving to find it. Aaron comes from a long line of movers and seekers. He is descended from one of seven Huntsman brothers who were part of a Catholic family that had come to America in 1641. The brothers were seized with the pioneering romance of fledgling Mormonism and joined the westward migration led by Brigham Young in the mid-1800s. One of the brothers,

Doyle Huntsman, took sick and was left behind in Iowa where he remained and became one of the founders of the town of Emerson. Others among the brothers who continued the journey were killed by Indians. Those who reached their destination became prominent in the Mormon community that formed Salt Lake City where the Huntsman name is still reverenced. Aaron jokes that restaurant staff in Salt Lake City always show him to the best table if he uses his name when making the reservation.

When Aaron tells you the story of his life, the details seem to blend and are reiterated differently with each telling. Family lore is always less about factual recording and more about the pride of traditions colorized and polished over generations. Aaron seems to have spent so much time moving from one place to another, the dates of each  transition are fuzzy even in his own mind. The listener soon learns not to worry about a careful chronology but to ride the crest of each chapter with the same sense of adventure —or sometimes resignation – that was central to his growing up. Aaron's own mother seemed to have inherited the family wanderlust. She gave birth to her only child on July 21, 1970 in Las Vegas, Nevada. She was unmarried at the time, and Aaron's father was a bad boy biker from Hollywood, California who fathered other children with other women concurrently. Aaron says that his mother tells him that when she was eight months pregnant, she answered a knock on the door and allowed Aaron's uninvited father to enter her home accompanied by his biker friends, all members of the Hell's Angels. She says that one of these men spoke to her, saying that she was the chosen one, that she should get her fur coat and a silver hairbrush given to her by her grandmother and that she should come with them to Death Valley. She looked up at the clock on the wall and saw that it had stopped. Every hair on her body stood up. She knew that she and her unborn child were in serious danger. Many years later she explained to Aaron that the man his father had brought to the house was Charles Manson who had given Aaron's father a Harley Davidson motorcycle for the right to sacrifice his unborn son. She said that Aaron's father continued to ride that bike until the day he died of a massive heart attack in 1984.

When the men left her home, Aaron's mother called her parents who placed her in hiding and paid Aaron's father enough money to keep him and Manson away from her.

When Aaron began to wonder about his father, he did some research that led him to the cemetery where he was interred. There, he found records that listed a son as a pall-bearer. Discovering he had a half-brother who was only six months his senior, Aaron contacted him and learned other details about their father.  His half-brother remembered a time when he and his father, doing a job for the Hell's Angels, burned down two gay bars – The Red Barn and The Gypsy – in Las Vegas. Upon learning this, Aaron, a bartender at the gay bar built on the site of The Gypsy, began to rethink his desire to meet this half-brother. They eventually did meet and have become good friends. Aaron's half-brother also told him that their dad was bisexual. Aaron has not yet learned how his half-brother came to know that.

Aaron's mother reacted to being terrorized by her boyfriend and his biker friends by embracing another religion with nineteenth century roots, the Jehovah's Witnesses. Aaron remembers going door to door with proselytizing church members until he was twelve years old. He says they would push him forward with an armful of brochures and a bible knowing that the person opening the front door would be less likely to slam it in the face of a cute kid.

In the mid '70s, Aaron's mother decided that a move to Oregon would be a good thing, but after a year there, the rainy climate depressed them both enough to make them move back to Las Vegas where Aaron's grandparents were beginning the construction of a family compound on 40 acres in an area now referred to as the Painted Desert golf community. At the time, Las Vegas was still a smallish place that was poised for booming expansion. Theirs was one of the first houses to be built in the area between Mount Charleston and Blue Diamond. What was then beyond city limits is now central Las Vegas. Aaron and his mother moved to the ranch where they became part of an extended family including cousins and uncles. His grandparents decided to try their hand at cattle ranching.

Aaron remembers an idyllic time spent hunting, fishing and hiking. Development soon caught up with them, and Aaron remembers an influx of Mormons. His grandparents tired of the cattle business after a few years and gradually sold off their ranch as building lots. Aaron says he had the impression that money was never an issue for him or his mother. There was always enough to keep him from ever having to worry about it, but more importantly, always enough to help him through any crisis he'd experience throughout his young life. Aaron's grandfather had been a racecar driver who transitioned to the automobile servicing business. He and Aaron's grandmother were engaged to be married on Valentine's Day. On his way to join his fiancée, he had stopped on the road to help fix a stranger's flat tire and was killed by a passing vehicle. His brother completed the task of collecting the bride-to-be and made her his own. There seems to be something in the Huntsman DNA that kept this family on an unmapped road to places they had not envisioned.

Aaron remembers those days of childhood in rural Las Vegas happily. His mother got a job working for the District Attorney who had his hands full dealing with the rampant crime and mob violence that were at the heart of the boom of adolescent Las Vegas. She and Aaron left the ranch and got an apartment across the street from Liberace's residence. Aaron remembers stepping into the street and almost being struck by a limousine. A bejeweled finger wagged at him through a lowered backseat window as Liberace yelled at him for jay walking. Later, Aaron's mother ruefully noted that had he been bumped by that limo, they'd have been on Easy Street for the rest of their lives.

Another frightening interaction that showed them the wild side of Las Vegas was a night when strangers woke them up, screaming and pounding on their front door, and demanding, "Is Jamie there? We know Jamie is in there!" This was followed by the sound of glass breaking at the backdoor. Four intruders entered their apartment. Aaron's mother says she remembers thinking that the Bible tells us that a woman threatened with rape is morally obliged to try to defend herself against the rapist. This she did with a hammer in hand. The intruders fled. The police eventually arrived and informed her that the intruders had gone down the street to another house where they attacked a couple, killing the husband and raping the wife.

A constant exposure to murder in unruly Las Vegas disturbed Aaron's mother who decided she and her son would relocate to Balboa Island in Newport Beach, California in 1982 where she would study court reporting. Her rationale for the move also included a desire for her son to be exposed to a better class of people and to get a taste of upper class living.

Aaron was in junior high school when they moved to Newport Beach. He remembers being a short kid who went from being 5'4" to 6'2" in less than one year, a growth spurt so fast and furious it had him writhing in pain in bed at night. (He is now 6'4".) Going through puberty did not mean, however, becoming sexually active. Aaron says, "I was a virgin until the night of my High School Senior Prom. Because I was a Jehovah's Witness, I didn't even jerk off until I was thirteen. I think maybe I had crushes on guys. I was looking at guys, and sometimes I'd get an erection but I always hid it. I never got caught. I acted like I was interested in girls throughout all my years of school. I always knew I was gay but I was in denial because I had been told that it was just something to do with not having a father. I probably got this idea from my mother who made sure I had plenty of adult males in my life to take his place as role models. At that time, my mother dated a man who eventually came out of the closet about six years ago. He and I were very close but he never came on to me or anything like that. Now he's 80 years old and I call him my 'Gay Dad.' We are still friends."

Aaron loved attending high school in Newport Beach, and he is proud of the fact that his school was one of the highest rated in the country. He remembers feeling discriminated against because of his dark hair in a largely blonde student body and because he was an outsider who was referred to as "Vegas." He says he wasn't invited to surf with the cool kids so he took up the boogie board and body surfing. He remembers being in the surf during one of the legendary New Zealand swells of 1986. Unable to reach the shore before being overtaken by a massive wave and dragged into it, he was watched by classmates on the beach who were sure he would not survive. After fighting the monster wave, he staggered out of the water with a broken board to the cheers of his classmates. This earned him their respect and friendship.

Aaron says that in high school he started to date girls seriously. He describes his dating as, "getting a six pack and then kissing. I had a habit of dating the girls that my guy friends had just broken up with. Not sure why. Of course, just when I was getting popular and secure, my mother announces that she wants to move again! I'm in my junior year. She tells me we are moving to Irvine which is about 20 miles south of where we were. This time, I threw a fit. We had a huge argument. She called me a bastard because I had no father. I answered, 'Well I know one thing. I'm a son of a bitch!' She tried to slap me but I broke it with my raised hand. This hurt her wrist and she threatened to call the cops claiming that I hit her. I ran away from home. I got on my bike and headed north. I made it all the way to Riverside. I called my grandparents and they sent me a plane ticket to Las Vegas. Once I was back in Vegas, my mom agreed that I should stay there and finish high school at Western High School. At Western, I started dating the most beautiful girls in the school. I did that because they were the ones who had the cutest boyfriends and that was what I was really after. Those guys would get mad at me because I was always stealing their girlfriends. I went to my Senior Prom with my high school sweetheart. She had broken up with a friend of mine and she was so pretty and I was thrilled that she said yes when I asked her to prom. I wore a white on white tux - because I was a virgin! That night we ended up back at her place and that's when she found out I was a virgin. That was some of the best sex I have ever had, and it was easy for me to fall in love with her. That night in the middle of sex, she asked me if I was gay. I denied it, but I could tell she had picked up on something. We were together for maybe ten months and we stayed friends until '89 when she got pregnant with someone else's baby. She didn't know what to do. She turned to me and I told her that if she wanted to keep the baby I would raise it with her. I proposed to her on the spot, and she accepted. I was serious about it, but a week later I get a phone call from her. She had an abortion. I dumped her. She wrecked me. I loved her and I would have loved her child and raised it as my own. When I was with her, I never thought about guys. Maybe it was my Jehovah's Witnesses upbringing but I couldn't understand how she could do such a thing. Her parents had a lot of money. They probably made her do it. I had become a part of her family, but I stopped talking to them all. It wasn't too long before she got pregnant again. Many years later, Lee and I ran into her when we had our one-year commitment ceremony. We were celebrating at the Flamingo Hilton and I spied her. I hadn't seen her for many years. She was still beautiful. I got up out of my seat to go talk to her but she ran out of the restaurant when she saw me. I guess it just wasn't meant to be. I wasn't a practicing Witness, and I wasn't going to church, but I felt that you just don't do a thing like abortion when you have someone who loves you and wants to love your child. I couldn't forgive her."

During high school, Aaron got a part-time job at Sizzler and also worked for his cousin who owned an electrical company. He got this first car, a Datsun, at sixteen, because his grandfather worked for Datsun-Nissan. (It is no surprise that a rolling stone true to his family DNA would put 200,000 miles on his first car despite being given two more cars at graduation.) Aaron says he finished high school "kicking and screaming." The one course he enjoyed was "Government," perhaps a predictor of a day later in life when he would sense the injustice of a legal system that treated him as a second-class citizen. He clashed with the teacher of that course who was ready to give him a failing mark that would have kept him from graduating, but he squeaked through with a grade high enough to allow him to graduate, with his Government teacher handing him his diploma. He was very surprised when, at graduation, his mother gave him her car and handed him a set of keys to her apartment in Irvine, California where she was still studying to become a court reporter. Aaron accepted the offer and drove west to resume living with his mother, but he was in for another surprise upon arrival. His mother had packed her bags. Aaron says, "She told me that she had not yet passed the tests required to become a court reporter, but she was accepting a job in New York City where a license in that field was not required. She said, 'Welcome to real life. The apartment is yours but you'll have to get a job to pay the rent.' The apartment was rent-subsidized because she was a student. I got a job at UC Irvine managing the gas station on campus. Here I am at age seventeen living on my own! This only lasted three months. I kind of screwed up. Nothing bad. Just what you'd expect from a kid. I didn't show up at work one day and I had the only keys to the gas station, so it threw the campus into a panic and I got fired. I was also informed that I would have to vacate the apartment. I did what I always did, call my grandparents. They sent one of my uncles who helped me get all my mother's things out of the apartment and brought to Las Vegas to be put into storage. I moved in with my mother's ex-boyfriend, the one who eventually came out of the closet and who I call my 'Gay Dad.' I went to work at his roofing company manning the phone. I also got a job at the Anaheim Arena waiting tables in the VIP section. That is when I began to get a sense of who the 'stars' were in California and I decided to become an actor. I took classes with Craig Campobasso, the famous casting director and acting coach. Two weeks into those classes, I'm cutting my hair, I'm doing improv, and I am coming out of the closet! Craig got me a part on 'Power Rangers' and in a movie called 'Beach Babes From Beyond'."

Aaron's "coming out" was not yet complete. He had a best friend in those years, an out-gay artist named Rick Stevens who bought into Aaron's straight charade. Aaron recalls Rick asking him to go to a gay bar with him. He says, "I told him 'Sure. Why not? It's not gonna bother me at all.' So we went to a bar called The Frat House. As soon as I walked through the door, I had a huge feeling of déjà vu. When I said this to Rick he said, 'Yeah, that's because you are a member of Sodom and Gomorrah.' I got really drunk that night. I was totally wrecked. I felt this was a sign from God. It threw me back into the closet for three months, but I kept thinking about that bar. I couldn't stay away. Finally, I went back there. Alone. When Rick found out, he was very angry with me. He was pissed because I had been lying to him about being straight – he had even known my girlfriend. He was also pissed because I didn't bring him with me when I went back to the bar. I felt bad about what I had done. Here is my best gay friend. He is my mentor. He was a world famous enamel artist who painted saints and angels. I still have many of his pieces. Rick died of pancreatic cancer many years later, but I think he is still with me in those paintings. They watch over me and protect me."

In addition to coming to terms with his sexuality, Aaron began to be aware of his good looks. He envisioned a modeling career. With the help of his acting coach, he enlisted a good photographer who produced his portfolio. He did some runway work in Los Angeles that got him offers from Zoli, Next, Wilhelmina and several other agencies that thought he had great potential. But Aaron's best friend, Rick, had returned to Las Vegas. Feeling unsure of himself, he gave up his job at the roofing company and his fledgling career as an actor, and followed his friend back to Las Vegas where he thought that armed with his photographs he might still get work as a model. He met a man named David Cervantes at a bar called "Angles and Lace" (which was adjacent to the gay bar his father burned down.) Aaron looks back on their year together wistfully, saying, "David was my first experience with Mexican culture and I was comfortable with it, but I was wild and not at all ready to settle down. Whenever I wanted to get out of a relationship like the one I had with David – who is still a good friend – I would blame my 'religious beliefs.' I got work in the casinos – I was a waiter at the Aladdin Hotel and Casino. I was enjoying life to the hilt. I was either traveling or going to a concert every weekend. I was making great money but as fast as I made it, I spent it. I did not have a gambling problem and I made sure all my bills were paid, but I wasn't saving anything. I was going everywhere and doing everything because I was in my early 20s and I was looking for something. I didn't know what I was looking for but I figured that if I kept going places I would find it."

His best friend Rick had a plan. He had heard that Key West, Florida was a mecca for gay artists. That is where he wanted to live, and he began to talk seriously about relocating. Aaron listened to him describe his dream and it almost matched his own fantasy of relocating to Miami Beach in order to advance his modeling career. He figured that once they were in Miami, Rick would forget all about continuing south to Key West. Under these less than perfectly honest premises, Aaron once again, gave up a fine job. Giving notice to his employer – the Aladdin Hotel – he sold everything and hit the road. Symbolic of their mismatched expectations, the two men drove to Florida in separate cars.

Aaron remembers their arrival in Miami Beach. He says, "We checked into the Tiffany which was a dive in those days. We hit the bars right away and got seriously drunk. Rick was encouraging me not to unpack too much because we were still not in Key West, which was his goal. I started wearing him down by saying how much fun it would be to stay in Miami Beach for a while. Well, we had two thousand dollars in traveler's checks that we brought down to the lobby of the Tiffany where we paid for our room for six months. I got a job at the Palace Bar and a second job at Burt Reynold's restaurant. I didn't have luck getting work as a model. I weighed 190 pounds and I would go to the gym and look at all these guys who were very muscular and I couldn't get there. I had no idea they were taking steroids to pump up. I also wasn't having any luck getting dates. I'd go to bars like Kremlin and Warsaw and I'd see those same muscle numbers dancing on the bars. Whenever I did meet someone, they always wanted to fuck first and talk later. That just wasn't me. The whole gay culture of Miami Beach and the wild circuit parties were just too much for me, so I left. I abandoned Rick. I drove back to my "security blanket," Las Vegas. I was lucky to get back my old job at the Aladdin."

This time, Aaron's career move seemed to result in more than a temporary job. He gained proficiency in restaurant operations at the Aladdin, but he remembers a difficult client who bested his patience, ending his career waiting tables. "A lady at one of my tables was bitching about clam chowder. She wanted something we did not have on the menu. She wouldn't let it go. Finally, I reached down into their breadbasket and grabbed a roll and shoved it into her mouth. Everyone at her table was a good sport about it, including the lady, but I was horrified with myself for doing that. After work, I went to the gay bar and sat at the bar telling the owner what had happened and how I felt that my time at the Aladdin would be over because of it. He asked me how old I was to be sure I was legal, and he offered me a job as a bartender on the spot. That is how I got into the career I still have."

While Aaron was enjoying his new career as a bartender in a Las Vegas gay bar, he got word that his best friend Rick had become seriously ill in Miami Beach. Pneumonia threatened his life, and Aaron managed to arrange Rick's return to Las Vegas. Their entire circle of friends assumed he was being brought home to die. Aaron and Rick had not discussed HIV/AIDS but now the disease had entered their life in a way that could not be ignored. With Rick in a hospital bed in Las Vegas, Aaron read about new life-saving drugs called protease inhibitors. He recalls rushing to Rick's bedside with the news, reminding him that he had medical insurance and would likely be a prime candidate to receive the new meds. Because the meds were not widely available in their first year, 1996, there seemed to be little chance for Rick to receive them fast enough to save his life. "I devoted all my energy to making sure that Rick got those new meds. I made a thousand phone calls to everyone I could, even to important people in DC. It worked, and Rick became the first person in Nevada to get the new meds and to survive."

With his best friend restored to health and with his new career as a bartender flourishing, Aaron might have finally settled into a long-term routine, but Rick followed through on his original dream of moving to Key West, and it was not long before Aaron once again gave up a good job, sold all his belongings and drove back to Florida in 1998 to be

with Rick. In Key West, Aaron, with his youthful good looks and experience, was attractive to the managers of the gay bars of Duval Street who promptly offered him work. Florida seemed finally to take root in his soul, as Aaron tended bar not just in Key West, but also in Fort Lauderdale, bouncing back and forth between the two communities and manning almost all the popular bars of those years including Cathode Ray, Twist and Boom. No matter how often he gave notice, there always seemed to be another venue that would be interested in his services. While not behind the bar, Aaron also studied real estate appraisal and kept that skill as back up for a day when he might not easily find work in a gay bar. That day never came.

Romance found him in Key West in the person of a well-known Key West entrepreneur who operated "Time Out" boat excursions, and was one of the stars in the pantheon of gay Key West in the '90s. The relationship was volatile.

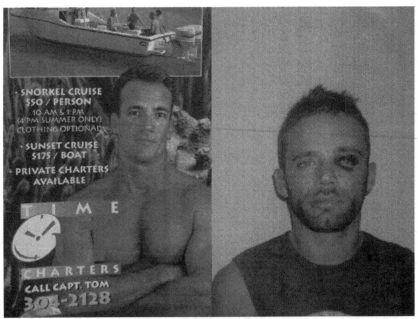

Aaron has photographs of the physical abuse he endured, and their relationship did not end well. This was an atypical situation for Aaron who is on good terms with almost everyone who has become a part of his life. Despite a difficult domestic situation, Aaron's professional life was successful. He was frequently featured on the covers of local publications, and he won the Mr. Key West Pride title in 2002, entitling him to compete in a national pageant in Atlanta. While backstage at the Mr. Hotlanta pageant, Aaron saw a stack of magazines ready for distribution and showing the winner's face on the cover. Realizing that the contest was fixed, he broke a few rules during the final runway event that would have gotten him disqualified. He had the last laugh, because a connection he made in Atlanta brought him back to Key West with a new gig. In 2003, he would become part of the team preparing for the premier unveiling of the "Sea-To-Sea" flag. Gilbert Baker, the flag's creator, had been asked to make a flag long enough to stretch the entire two and one quarter mile length of Duval Street, connecting the Atlantic Ocean to the Gulf of Mexico. The installation of this flag became an historic Key West event, but returning to Key West to work on this project turned out to be personally significant for Aaron. Upon his return, he walked into Bourbon Street Pub where he had once tended bar. The sight of a man behind the bar made him forget everything else. He immediately asked anyone within reach for information about the man and for an introduction. His name was William Lee Jones. Aaron Huntsman knew in a flash that he had finally found what he was looking for.

WILLIAM LEE JONES

A slow three-mile drive down Main Street in the West Virginia steel town of Weirton, hard by the Ohio River and in a northern panhandle sandwiched between Ohio and Pennsylvania, will help you understand William Lee Jones. Weirton is a no-nonsense town where the dreary one or two-story brick-faced buildings of Main Street tell you that here you will find practical people of modest expectations. Their churches are the tidiest buildings on Main Street. Their shops form a repeating pattern of hardware and bar. Sensible trucks form most of the Main Street traffic, and those trucks define the citizens of Weirton more than do their dreams. It was demise of his truck that inadvertently brought Lee to Aaron.

William Lee Jones was born in Weirton on May 23, 1971. He has a brother one year older, and would be followed four and half years later by a sister. To describe his father as hard-working would be an understatement. When he wasn't at work in the steel mill, he was running the 89 acre family farm or serving the town as a volunteer fireman. Although he never pressed Lee to follow his career at the steel mill, he taught by example the personal satisfactions of a productive life.

Lee acquired the common wisdom of a solid public school education. His parents were not particularly strict or demanding. When Lee is asked what religion he was raised in, he shrugs and explains that it all depended on which he friend he might be going to church with on any Sunday. Although he describes his parents as "old school farmers," they were not particularly liberal or conservative, but were definitely open-minded. Lee regrets never having come out to his parents who died within five months of each other several years ago. When he spoke of this regret to his sister, her response startled him. She said, "Oh they knew. We all knew. You don't go through high school without a single date and without even one girlfriend without making it obvious. And we knew Aaron wasn't just your 'business partner' because nobody stays with his business partner after the business dies, and moves all over the country with him. Yeah, they knew."

She was right about the no-girlfriend thing. Lee explains that he never "had feelings" for girls. His youth was not romantic. He would come home from school and go right out to work in the fields. The chores of taking care of horses and cows and chickens kept the family occupied. If anyone even noticed that Lee did not seek out the company of girls, there was no mention of it. Did Lee have feelings for boys? He says, "I kind of had an inkling that I might be headed in that direction when I was a freshman in high school. There was a junior in my Spanish class. He was the star of the football team and built like a brick shithouse. I had a huge crush on him. Never did anything about it, but a year after he graduated, I found out he was gay." That was probably every gay man's story growing up gay in a town like Weirton in the '80s. No internet cruising, no bars, no Pride parades. As Lee puts it, "Ain't many places to meet guys up there in the hills of West Virginia. I didn't really get into the scene until I moved to Key West in 2002."

How did Lee envision his future while growing up in Weirton? He says he was content where he was, and that he never felt like Dorothy in Kansas yearning to find a place somewhere over the rainbow and far away. "I was happy

living on the farm. I didn't feel like I was missing something. I had friends who were fire fighters. My dad and my older brothers were volunteer fire fighters, and I got into it at 16 when there was a huge wild fire. They needed help containing it, and I asked my dad if I could come with him. I loved it. I was hooked."

Like his father, Lee filled every waking moment with productive activity. When not at school, or working the farm or at the firehouse, he was also active in 4H throughout high school. Lee envisioned a future as either a landscape architect or perhaps a math teacher. He chose the landscape architecture program at University of West Virginia, informing his parents that he would not enroll unless he could pay for it himself. He still feels strongly that because kids are the ones who will benefit from their education, they ought to be the ones to pay for it, rather than their parents, even if that means working extra jobs which is what he planned to do throughout college. After two weeks at UWV, he found out that his parents had

mortgaged the family farm in order to pay for his college education. He immediately cancelled the loan, returned the funds to the bank and called his parents to come and bring him home. Back in Weirton, Lee shifted gears. The local community college did not offer a degree in landscaping, so he pursued his alternate goal of becoming a math teacher. Lee describes his awakening in the course of those studies. "I was just one credit away from my teacher certification when I admitted to myself that I did not want to spend my life in a classroom trying to teach a bunch of unruly and undisciplined kids who didn't want to learn. I just didn't like kids who were out of control in the classroom."

While in college, he continued his work as a volunteer fire fighter. This evolved in the direction of paramedical experience. He started associating with the ambulance squad, leading him to a year and a half of training at the community college to get West Virginia certification as an EMT. He then went to Ohio to acquire an advanced EMT certification. After a year and a half of schooling, he became a licensed paramedic. He was in his mid-20s, feeling he had found his career, still living at home and guarding his secret gay identity without much anxiety. Lee just assumed that is what gay men did. He says he did have one or two gay friends in those years. One of them owned a video rental shop that had a special "room in the back" for adult videos including a gay-themed rack. He says he was careful never to let shoppers see him inspect that rack. His neighbors must have been careful too. Lee says he never met anyone else at that rack. His Weirton life was non-sexual and decidedly unromantic, a circumstance that would not change until his eventual move to Key West.

His work as a firefighter and paramedic continued for fourteen years, finally taking him out of Weirton. He says, "In 2000, I applied to go to California to join the Bureau of Land Management as part of the crew on one of their wild lands firefighting trucks. I went out there for two years and fought fires up and down the coast of California. I became the head lineman. In my second year, they sent me to a US Forest Service Engine Academy where I had to gain skills involving complete knowledge of the truck and its operation. There were obstacle courses that had to be mastered. I placed second in the class, and was an assistant engineer during my second season in California. After that season, I came home on break. One day, I was in my truck when some guy blew through an intersection and slammed into me. Tore off the front end of the truck. I was about a mile from the firehouse I worked at. I was injured but I called it in myself. The firefighters and ambulance crew that arrived were all people I knew. The guy who hit me kept whining that he had to get to the airport. That didn't go over well with the police."

Because of the accident, Lee had knee surgery and a persistent back injury requiring ongoing attention. The initial therapy took six months. During this time, Lee decided to do something he had never before considered. He says, "I had never taken a vacation. I had heard about this place called Key West and I just made a quick decision to go there for fifteen days. I loved it right away. I talked with the guys at the fire department there, showed them all my credentials, and they told me that I had more certifications than anyone they had working there. It looked like I'd be working with them until they told me that they wanted to send me back to school for additional training. I was 31 years old. I'd be older than all the other students. I couldn't do that. I declined the job. So, I said to myself, 'I'll be a bartender. Why not?' I asked the manager of Bourbon Street Pub for a job, and he started me as a bar-back. I remember thinking that I was having so much fun, and that if things worked out fine, but if not, fine. It was an easier career for me because it didn't have the life-or-death stress that comes with being a paramedic where people are dying on you."

Never the slouch and quick to make bartender friends, Lee learned the art of mixing drinks from buddies who would pull him behind the bar to teach him everything he would need to know to do their job. He was swiftly becoming part of the fabric of Key West, but he remained single. He says, "Romance? Not really. There were a couple of guys I got close to and hung around with, but no one sparked my interest until that night when Aaron walked into the bar. I had been working at the bar for six months as a bar-back. Aaron was in Key West working on a project for Absolute Vodka and the Sea-to-Sea gay flag event. It was 2003. Another bar-back said, "You have an admirer. He pointed to Aaron. My friends all tried to run interference because he was intense about it. They were telling him I already had a boyfriend but it didn't stop him. Finally, Donny, one of the older bartenders and a bookkeeper for the bar gave in to Aaron and introduced us. He did a Key West handshake on me and I about had a heart attack. [The Key West handshake consists of extending a hand but shaking the crotch of the person to whom you are introduced.] We hit

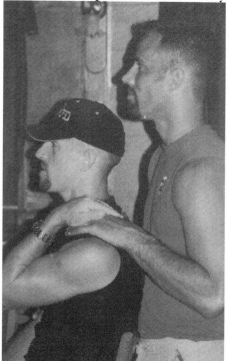

it off right away. We have been together ever since. Soon enough, we were both bartenders at the same place, working different shifts. When one of us was off work, he'd be sitting at the other one's bar. Even with that, we were able to separate our business relationship from our personal relationship. Bars don't always like hiring couples because if the relationship has problems, the bar feels it. We didn't have those problems. I remember the second night after we met, I was living in a room in the employee housing above the bar. Aaron said he was tired and wanted to sleep, so I sent him upstairs to my room while I finished my shift. While he was in my room, he discovered all my firefighter gear. At the end of the night, as I am climbing the stairs, I could smell that 'house fire' smell that you can never get out of your gear. I opened the door to my room and I found him all tricked out in my gear. Yup, found a firefighter in my bed. It was a hot time in the old town that night."

Lee was finally up against a fire he did not want extinguished.

ATTORNEY BERNADETTE RESTIVO

The saga of marriage equality in Florida is really the story of an unlikely coalition of folks with diverse histories but matching hearts. Perhaps the most amazing aspect of the Huntsman-Jones victory over the sad legacy of homophobic Anita Bryant is that it took a Catholic straight woman lawyer who had been a powerful leader in the Republican party to make things right!

Attorney Bernadette Restivo, like her clients Huntsman, and Jones, came to Florida looking for a personal reinvention. She comes from Toledo, Ohio and is the daughter of a judge. She was raised a very liberal Democrat. Because of her family influences, she came to activism easily. She says, "I did all the marches. At school in Washington, DC, I was with 'Americans for Democratic Action.' I was always politically active. I started campaigning for candidates at the age of ten. I always wanted to run for office and become the first female President. I would say my evolution away from the Democratic politics of my upbringing was not immediate. I was, at one time, an elected Democratic official – a state central committee woman. I had gone to American University in Washington, graduating in 1982 with a concentration in communications, economics and political science. I came home and started law school that Fall at the University of Toledo. I was clerking for a Democrat judge, but I got married that year and decided that a legal profession was not for me. I dropped out of law school much to my father's chagrin, and I started my family. Having had a son in 1984, I decided to go back to school to get an MA in Public Administration. I had my daughter at the same time I was graduating. I then spent ten years as alumnae and development director and alumni director at my high school alma mater. In all, I had spent 16 years of my life with the Sisters of Notre Dame. They are in Toledo, Ohio. They were my teachers and subsequently, my employers. I was brought up as a devout Roman Catholic. Those sisters were wonderful ladies. I'm sure they are none too pleased with my pro-marriage equality stance, but I have spoken with some of them who have privately given me the 'thumbs up.' I had my third child, a daughter, while I was working at their academy. When she turned five, I decided to go back to law school. I had her on one knee and my Civil Procedure text book on the other knee."

A few years before reigniting her time in law school, Restivo had gotten divorced, and had married Tom Noe, a prominent Ohio Republican. She says, "Our political affiliations were so different. I had what I used to call a 'mixed marriage' with him being the head of the Republican party in our county in Ohio. I had my first marriage annulled by the Catholic Church, and because of my beliefs as a Roman Catholic, specifically in the matter of abortion, I eventually left the Democrats, and slowly converted to the Republicans. I think some people get more conservative as they get older, and that was what happened to me. I had always been a fiscal conservative."

For a while, both Restivo and Noe had great tandem careers in Ohio Republican politics. They were stellar fund-raisers for the 2004 Bush-Cheney ticket, and became friends of those successful candidates, until a media-fueled scandal known as "Coingate" put an end to their political aspirations and resulted in incarceration for Tom Noe who is now serving a multi-year sentence. Restivo recalls those anguished days with the steady voice of a survivor. "As George Bush began his 2004 re-election campaign, Tom became the Bush coordinator for the upper left quadrant of Ohio. I got elected county party chair. We accomplished a lot. I raised a lot of money. I think I was successful. We were becoming a threatening force. It had started with our work on the gubernatorial campaign in 2002. We were now going to places like the White House Christmas party. The President knew us. He called me 'Bernie.' Our success angered a lot of people. In 2005, they came after Tom. He was accused of campaign funding irregularity and of mismanagement of state funds. An Ohio newspaper eventually won a journalism prize for hounding us. At that point, my children were still relatively impressionable. I had to take them out of that caustic environment. We had acquired a home in Florida in 1998, so I brought the kids down there in 2005. It was an awful time. I still have PTSD. There were helicopters and boats with cameras. I think they actually published photos of my son in his underwear. We were hunted. My life was thrown into chaos."

Restivo and Noe divorced in 2009. While they drifted apart, Restivo did her best to keep the children – Noe's two daughters, and Restivo's three children - intact as a family unit with their father in prison. Noe and Restivo are now in communication and trying to see if there might be some way to become close again.

In Florida, Restivo (like Huntsman, Jones and Ebenhoch) had to reinvent herself. "I had graduated law school in 1999. Politics was my primary profession. I had very little experience as a practicing lawyer. In Ohio, I had a talk show ready to air on the local FOX affiliate. I had a newspaper column and a radio show lined up. All that fell apart. I had taken the Ohio bar in 2000, and at the time, maybe because we already had the place down here, I took the Florida bar in 2001, never thinking I'd practice law down here. The little bit of practicing I did in Ohio was child advocacy work and family law. That was my interest. About a month after we got down to the Florida Keys, I saw that the "Guardian Ad Litem" program [Giving a voice in court to children and infants in dependency cases, the Guardian Ad Litem expresses their wishes.] was looking for a lawyer. This was custom-made for me and I did that job for about a year until DCF [Department of Children and Families] recruited me to be their lawyer. After that, I went to work for a solo practitioner for a year, opened up my own law firm in Key Largo, turned it into a partnership with Jessica Reilly, brought on Elena Vigil-Farinas. Now it's just me and Elena."

How did this devout Catholic, Republican, straight mother of three come to defend Huntsman and Jones in their fight for marriage equality in Florida? Restivo explains, "My law partners and I were sitting in our conference room reading about all the states where anti-gay marriage laws were falling, and we were wondering why this wasn't moving ahead in Florida and how much we would love to handle a case like that, so we contacted Tom Hampton who was Of Counsel to our firm and was a gay man living in Key West. We asked if there was anyone who would like to bring that case, and he knew Aaron and Lee and set up a meeting at his house. There were a couple of other Florida couples at that meeting but Aaron and Lee were the only ones at that point who had the courage to pull the trigger."

Restivo remembers devising a plan that had to involve not just her clients, but the other marriage equality legal actions that were percolating elsewhere in Florida and across the country. "So you ask what was the first step? To study the cases in the other states. I am also licensed in Ohio and I had been following the Obergefell case. I was reading all the briefs and it seemed to me that from state to state the briefs were looking very similar, so writing our brief wasn't that difficult, as the strategy behind the whole thing was clear to me. We set up a network of attorneys across Florida and across the nation, and we were exchanging information and research and briefs, so that everybody would stay consistent. You wouldn't want arguments all over the map. At that point, Equality Florida had an attorney who was coordinating the arguments in Florida and he was very helpful. He stopped us from making a huge strategy mistake, and put us in touch with the attorneys in Miami. This involved making more of a federal argument within our case that would have allowed the AG to remove our case and take it out of Tallahassee. As far as competitiveness goes, we were all doing this work for free. I don't think anyone thought that this would bring any notoriety to any of us and we weren't trying to one-up each other at that point. And then the media explosion happened. I mean, we hoped, - not for our own notoriety but for Aaron and Lee - that their case would get noticed.

The media explosion meant we took on a whole other section of work. I think at the time there was a sort of 'race to the courthouse' with our complaint because it was about the same time Equality Florida filed their case."

Restivo knew she would need to craft her case with the most effective and winning arguments and strategies that had been used elsewhere. A misstep in the initial crafting of the case could have crippled it many junctures, including the appeal process. She explains her thinking about her choice of approach. "What were the arguments I thought would be strongest? That's a good question, and you have to realize we were up against a conservative Catholic judge, Judge Luis Garcia. However, Judge David Audlin, who was a gay judge, was the original judge assigned to the case. He was the judge who first ruled in favor of gay adoption in Florida, but he never got notoriety for that decision because there was no appeal. Immediately after the case got assigned to him, he was personally attacked. He was attacked ethically and morally, and he resigned from the bench. Did anyone put two and two together and think this attack happened because he got assigned to this case? We lost a really good judge, and then the case went into limbo and it had to be reassigned and we got a memo in May that all Judge Audlin's cases would be reassigned in July, and we panicked and thought 'No, no, no, we can't wait until July 1st just to get a reassignment. So we filed an emergency motion for an assignment, and we wrote a compelling brief about how Aaron and Lee's constitutional rights could not wait that long. That is how we got reassigned by Chief Circuit Judge Garcia who took the case himself."

Was Restivo worried about her case being assigned to a conservative Catholic judge? "No, because at that point we were appearing almost exclusively before Judge Garcia in our family practice. He was the only circuit judge in the Upper Keys. Elena's been there for 20+ years and me for at least ten and we have a good rapport with him. We have a professional respect for each other and we knew we would get a fair hearing. As the other states started to fall, it looked good and it looked like we had a compelling case. And as the opposition filed amicus briefs - and they were more and more ridiculous with every filing - we felt like the home team. We felt confident because we were on our own turf in a courtroom where we were well known and comfortable. I never anticipated losing. As far as the arguments go, it was to us a no-brainer from a constitutional perspective. The thing for us was to present the right argument in anticipation of an appeal, which we were certain was inevitable. Look how fast our case moved - from April 1, 2014 when we filed it to July 17, 2014 when we got a decision! We thought it might be a year-long wait! The opinion of Judge Garcia was very detailed and scholarly."

Restivo says that Aaron and Lee's case became her fulltime job and consumed her legal practice. She and her law partner joked that they should have gotten jobs at Starbucks just to keep some money coming into the firm while Restivo worked on the case. After the decision, Restivo joined the ranks of those who succumb to the siren-call of Key West. She has moved her practice from Key Largo to the Conch Republic for a number of reasons. "Why did I move to Key West? The truth is that Key Largo has very little for a single woman. It's rather slow. Not a lot to do. I love all the people there, but I like the central city feel of Key West. The whole city is a neighborhood. I thought that because I spent so much time here with Aaron and Lee and made so many lifelong friends that I wanted to be near them. I always say to Mark Ebenhoch 'If you were a straight man I'd marry you.' We hit it off. And when my Key Largo house sold, I moved in with him for a while, and Aaron thinks of me as his surrogate mother! Getting to know them showed me that this would be a good area of law to practice. I always wanted to help. I had to sell my house anyway, so I thought where do I want to be? I did become a Democrat again along the way. When Catherine Vogel ran for State Attorney, I became a Democrat for her. In Key Largo, I was active in my Catholic church. I was a cantor at my church in Tavernier. I am still an active Catholic. I love being a Catholic. People know who I am and what I stand for, but we are all sinners and most people stray a bit from the teachings of the Church in some area. As to the issue of same-sex marriage, the Pope said 'Who am I to judge?'"

Restivo is fearless about her unclear future. "We are going through a real transition with the firm. Trying to downsize in Key Largo and focus more in Key West. I am going through a difficult time professionally. Truthfully, I spent way too much time on a case that didn't pay us anything. I don't regret it, but it took its toll on the firm. I hope ultimately it will open up more opportunities. I am toying with going back into the non-profit sector, I was always one of those do-gooders who isn't happy unless she is helping someone. At 55, I still have so much time ahead of me. I always tell my kids nobody has to be one thing for your whole life. I will know what I will do next when it finds me. I love practicing law but you can do that in a variety of ways."

Restivo's family is wholeheartedly cheering her on. "My kids are very creative. My son is California software developer. My middle daughter is a professional singer, yoga instructor/vegan, my little one is 25 and is in retail management at Disney. They are all proud of me. I have to say, my 91 year-old mother is very impressed with me. We call her Saint Jane because she's as Catholic as they get, and I showed her pics of me and Aaron and Lee and a video of one our TV interviews on my Ipad, and she said 'Well I can understand. I guess everyone needs a partner, so they should be allowed to get married.' You could have knocked me over with a feather. My dad died just about two years ago. I looked up to him a lot, not just as a judge with a great legal mind but as my dad. The morning we were getting ready to file Aaron and Lee's suit, I got woken up at 4:30AM by 'Joy To The World.' I'm laying in bed and I hear 'Joy To The World' and I think I am dreaming. I had a roommate at the time and I went downstairs and said 'Did you hear Joy To The World?' She thought I was crazy. A few days later, in a bureau drawer in my bedroom I found a card that my father had sent. It was one of those cards that when you pull the tab on it, plays a song. That song was 'Joy To The World.' No way in the world would that just have gone off by itself. I took it as a great sign that I was about to do something very important."

In Key West, Restivo continues to follow her heart. She has become active in animal rescue, and recently sang her way to a victory in the popular singing competition, Aqua Idol, held at the club where Aaron tends bar. With Aaron, Lee, Mark and the others who formed the team that ended Anita, Restivo has found a place in what Key West calls its "One Human Family."

THE MANHUNT SCANDAL OF JUDGE DAVID AUDLIN

Someone hated and persecuted Florida 16th Circuit Chief Judge David Audlin, but in an odd twist of fate, his resignation over a Manhunt profile did more for marriage equality in Florida than he could have accomplished if he had heard the case himself.

Over breakfast at Island House in Key West, David Audlin tells me that he has never really explained his resignation from the bench and that he is glad for this opportunity to reveal the truth.

David Audlin grew up in Syracuse, New York, studied Philosophy and History, dabbled in acting and, drawn by its good weather, moved to Los Angeles where he went to law school at USC, becoming a commercial litigator for three years. He had already come out of the closet in Provincetown on his 20th birthday. He remembers those years as being a kind of pre-AIDS gay paradise. "We were enjoying the post-Stonewall sexual freedom before all the troubles started. Everyone was having a ball, with the assumption that there was nothing we couldn't fix with a shot of penicillin."

Audlin was living with a boyfriend in West Hollywood when they heard Key West described as "Ptown only bigger and better." They did not simply visit Key West, they moved there, buying property in "Old Town," and transforming it into a gay guesthouse which they named after a Los Angeles gay bar, the Blue Parrot.

Audlin took a big cut in pay when he moved to Key West. In California, he had been part of a white glove firm doing the kind of commercial litigation in which "you never actually went to court." Audlin recalls his job interview with that firm. "I always say I was raised as a lawyer by Jews and Italians. I was called into their offices to talk about a job offer they had for me. Usually, these offers are made by lower level people, but the partners themselves wanted to interview me. At the conclusion of our meeting, as I was getting up to leave, they said there was one more thing they wanted to discuss with me, that some of the partners had mentioned that I was gay. They wanted me to know that if that were true, they were okay with it. One of the heads of the firm said he remembered what it was like to have doors closed to him because he was Jewish. Another one said he remembered what it was like to have doors closed to him because he was Italian. I was grateful for their understanding and it was great to work in a place that was free of homophobia."

Audlin says that his Key West practice was very different from his LA work. "I found myself working in the Public Defender's office, learning how to be a 'real' lawyer. I tried things like gritty little DUI cases that helped people who would vomit on your shoes. In those days, Key West had a 1970s jail that had been purchased in Texas, cut into two sections and brought over on a barge from Galveston. It was decrepit even then, like a tiny version of the Bastille with bare bulbs hanging from the ceiling and water running down the walls. I'd have to go there to meet with my clients. This was my new life as a lawyer. At the same time, we were having a good time running our guesthouse. In 1987, my partner died of AIDS. I took care of him without much help because in those days nobody understood the vector of the disease, and nobody was even really sure he had the disease because the testing process was new. Somehow, I made it through that minefield of AIDS in those early days."

After his partner's death, Audlin sold his Key West guesthouse and moved to Maine. He describes losing a second lover to AIDS. "Darrell was a sweet man. He was from Georgia, the thirteenth child in his family and the best looking boy you have ever seen. I was 29 and he was 22, so there wasn't much age difference between us, but we figure he had contracted HIV when he was 14. He died when he was 23."

Audlin returned to Florida to work at the Office of the Attorney General in Tallahassee. In 1996, he returned to Key West. He says, "I hung out my shingle and made a freaking ton of money with a solo practice where I would help anyone who walked in the door. The lawyers up north remembered me, and the judges remembered me, so I got great referrals. Business was good, but after awhile, I began to think it would be interesting to be a judge because there are so few liberal ones in Florida which remains a very conservative state.

I don't mean to sound pious about becoming a judge given that I took a huge cut in pay to do it, but I really did have a sense of obligation to the legal system. I was a good litigator and my lawyer friends urged me to consider it. In addition to reduced income, I gave up the freedom you have in private practice to make your own hours and to come and go whenever and wherever you want. A judge is after all a state employee. When a retirement produced an opening, my lawyer friends nominated me and I ran unopposed twice. I was elected in 2006 and re-elected in 2012. They sent me to "baby judge school" where we learned how to handle the courtroom, the gavel, and how not to trip on your robes because you really do look awfully silly if you fall. This was vastly different from the training I received to become a commercial litigator where they just wanted to make sure I knew how to eat in polite company."

Audlin says that because he had always had an out-and-proud life, he was not going to go into the closet after becoming a judge. In Key West, he continued to socialize at gay establishments such as Island House where people knew his name and that he had a partner, Frank Alvarez, with whom he has been together for 17 years.

About his relationship with Alvarez, Audlin says, "During our first ten years together, we were monogamous. Although we have not formally married, I consider Frank to be my husband. I'm not denigrating anyone who wants that marriage certificate but to me it's a contract about money. I remember talking with my first lover about marriage. He said that in some ways people get lazy when they think they have you bound by a legal obligation like marriage. He said that without it, you are on your best behavior. When I met Frank I was frustrated with being single. I wasn't meeting anyone down here in Key West, so I went to a party in Miami where an ex-boyfriend named Evan brought Frank as his date. Here was this beautiful Cuban guy with my ex, and I knew it would never work out for them and I said to Frank, 'When you're done seeing

Evan, I'd love to see you.' We moved in together six months later. Frank was the most important part of the decision I made to resign my judgeship."

Audlin says that his early years as a judge were enjoyable. He was learning a new trade in which he was often like a policeman/referee. There are in the workday of a judge long periods of tedium which Audlin describes as, "like doing long division" but there are also those fascinating cases that make up for the routine. Audlin says, "My primary area was civil law, but I also heard juvenile and family law cases. I was conservative in my decisions on the criminal justice side where I think people expected more leniency from me, but as a public defender, I had seen so many serious physical injuries and permanent handicaps as a result of felony drunk driving that I would lower the boom on them. If the person convicted had connections in town, my popularity would suffer, but I did what I thought was right, and you know, if there are two people standing in front of me, one is going to win and one is going to lose. I was very careful never to embarrass a lawyer in front of a client because I knew what that felt like after my many years of practice. I had many lawyer friends and they saw to it that when I was up for re-election, I again ran unopposed."

In 2008, Judge Audlin ruled in favor of gay adoption rights, effectively dismantling Florida's long-standing and unique state prohibition that had its roots in the Anita Bryant hysteria. The case involved Wayne LaRue Smith and his partner who had been foster parents to many needy children. Smith now wished to formally adopt a child who wanted to be able to call him dad. Florida Attorney General Bill McCollum and DCF both declined to appeal the case.

Audlin recalls, "I don't think any of the other circuit court judges really wanted the case. It was a hot potato. When it ended up with me, I held a full two-week evidentiary bench trial in which the State was invited to defend the anti-adoption statute but they chose not to. The kind of full trial I conducted makes a ruling much better able to stand up against an appeal, but there was no appeal. I had given some thought as to whether I should take myself off the case. For the record, I formally disclosed that I was gay. But the best guidance I got was from the example and words of black Federal Judge A. Leon Higginbotham, Jr. who wrote that a judge should not recuse himself from a case just because he is a member of a minority group. He should recuse himself only if he has already made up his mind about a case before hearing it. If, as a gay judge, I have an open mind and come to my ruling based on the evidence I hear, I am acting appropriately."

Audlin relied on the US Constitution's ban on "bills of attainder" (laws enacted specifically to penalize or punish a specific person or class of persons.) He thought it was clear that Florida's 1977 ban on gay adoption fell into that category of injustice.

Because of his ruling on the gay adoption case, Audlin was contacted by Equality Florida, asking if he would be willing to be honored at a gala to be held in Key West. Audlin accepted the offer and the event was publicized in south Florida newspapers. Shortly before the gala, Audlin received a phone call from an appellate judge on the west coast of Florida who was a member of the Judicial Ethics Advisory Committee. That judge said that he had been informed that Audlin was planning to attend an event where funds would be solicited, making his presence a serious violation of judicial ethics. Although Audlin did not agree with the judge's warning, given that Equality Florida was not the kind of organization targeted by the prohibition, he canceled out of the event. He put the experience out of his mind, but recollected it when he got a call from a judicial assistant within the Judicial Qualifications Commission, (JQC) saying that they had received a complaint about a posting of a personal profile on a site called *Manhunt*. Audlin says, "Someone had apparently tipped off the JQC that a gay judge had a profile on Manhunt. They asked me if it was my profile and if I had created it. I never denied it. That profile was not shocking or particularly sexy. It was funny more than anything else. There was some kind of self-appointed judicial watchdog blog out of Miami that was making a huge deal out of it, claiming that this was shocking and inappropriate. It seems this same source had sent the information to the Miami Herald and to the Key West Citizen. When the papers did not consider the tip to be newsworthy, the complainer brought it to the JQC. The JQC's actions were never made public because I stepped down before they had to do anything. The case was sealed. Most people are not aware of all this because of that. This is the first time I am talking about it. When the JQC began its inquiry, I lawyered up to prepare a defense. Lawyers close to me knew about the situation, but the public did not. My lawyers asked the JQC why this profile on Manhunt was different from any other profile such as one that might be placed on match.com or even christianmingle.com. The JQC was of the opinion that my Manhunt profile would somehow constitute behavior that would bring the judiciary into disrepute. It turns out that the judge who had warned me not to attend the Equality Florida gala was also a member of the JQC! Through my lawyers, I learned that the JQC had already made up its mind – without hearing any evidence – that my behavior was inexcusable. I began to see the kind of trial I'd get by that kangaroo court which was acting more like a lynch mob than anything else. In fact, one of my lawyers called my situation a 'gentile lynching.'

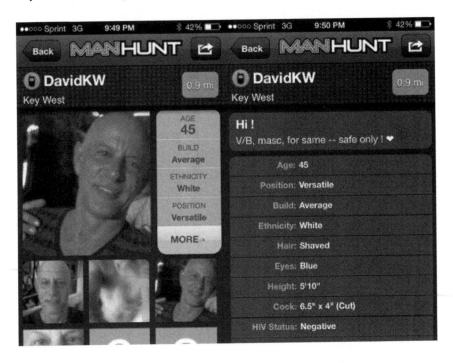

Huntsman v. Heavilin attorney Bernadette Restivo feels that this attack on Audlin, coming concurrently with her filing of their marriage equality case was no coincidence. It was obvious that the case would go to Judge Audlin who concurs with her suspicions, saying, "I think she's right, given the warnings I had received and then the comments made by Republican-appointed members of the JQC who had made up their minds on the issue, and had found out that the Huntsman v Heavilin case had been assigned to me. I guess those judges thought that I had made up my mind about marriage equality in Florida just like they had made up their minds about me before even looking at the evidence. I honestly don't know what I would have done with that marriage case if I had heard it. I can only speculate about which way I would have ruled but it would have been based on what was presented to me."

Because of those complaints to the JQC, Judge Audlin retired from the bench and the marriage equality case went to the straight, conservative Monroe County Chief Circuit Judge Luis Garcia. Audlin says he admires Garcia's ruling on the case and thinks he himself would have reached the same conclusions.

Audlin recalls the extreme stress and anxiety he had deciding whether to fight the JQC or to resign from the bench. He says, "It was a miserable time for me. Look, I did the math. I talked it over and over with my partner Frank. It occurred to me that I wanted my life back. I wanted *our* life back. Were these threats going to continue? Was I going to become the object of constant attacks, and would I always have to look over my shoulder whenever I was here having a drink at Island House or putting a dollar tip in a dancer's shorts? I knew how to keep my personal and professional life separate, and I hadn't even identified myself as a judge on that Manhunt profile. My lawyers were very disappointed with my decision to resign. They kept saying, 'David, don't do this. We are going to let the people persecuting you find out that you are a good judge.' Part of my decision was personal but part of it was my desire to protect the court from an ongoing mess. To become embroiled in a pissing match with the conservative JQC where I knew I'd probably lose, and then to have to spend a couple of hundred thousand dollars to bring the case to the Florida Supreme Court that might also rule against me was a bad option. Also, if they ruled against me it would set a very bad precedent for any gay judge coming after me. The JQC wanted a highly visible spectacle. They wanted this to play out publicly. I wasn't about to give them that kind of lynching. I had been proud to be a judge. I was grateful for the opportunity to use my ability and experience to help people and to give something back to the community. I had been well-rewarded as a lawyer. I looked down the road at the three and a half years left in my term. I would have to spend at least half of that litigating my own case. That would have put my partner through a miserable time, and the whole thing could have ended with a disaster. I also knew what that situation would do to the Huntsman v Heavilin marriage equality case. Whoever was persecuting me was doing it in order to fight marriage equality. You know some gay men live their lives in a very gay world, whereas some of us venture out into the straight world as openly gay men and this is the price we sometimes pay."

David Audlin is now happily enjoying the good life with his partner in Key West. Maybe it was the strong coffee served poolside at Island House that made Audlin release a torrent of words both reflective and forward-thinking in his assessment of what had befallen him. As I listened to him, I began to realize why so many smart men stay out of politics and public sector jobs, leaving those important responsibilities to others with lesser intuitions and capabilities, and whose main qualification might be the fact that their sex lives are innocuous, insipid and boring.

Audlin summed up his story saying, "The upshot is that I have the rest of my life to enjoy. I was able to retire early, and now I'm just plain happy. I read. I travel. I have a great looking husband. I'm on vacation for the rest of my life and still living in Key West. I've been very successful. I don't need to practice law. I'm not bored with law, and maybe someday I will practice again but not right now."

I had a final question for Audlin. I told him that in listening to his story, I began to suspect that there was something more than just that Manhunt profile that had come to light. I doubted that there would have been such a reaction to just that profile. I asked him if the JQC had anything else on him that he had not disclosed to me. Had he ever been caught somewhere with his pants down? His answer was clear. "No, that's all they had. The Manhunt profile had a picture of me without a shirt. The reaction of the JQC was like something out of a French farce. When you hear the story from the outside, it sounds like there must be more, but there was nothing else. Even my friends who are lawyers said 'Look it's going to leave the impression that there's more here than the Manhunt profile.' To be frank, one reason for my resignation was that I didn't want to piss in the soup for the next person who wants to be a gay judge. I didn't want to leave a big mess. I didn't want to discourage people who would then say 'Why should I put my neck on the line? I'll stay in private practice and make a lot of money.' The Manhunt profile was all the JQC had. I told them that it wasn't even a technical violation and that they should dismiss the case. That is really what should've happened. Should I have been more discreet? I don't know. You know, I'm a gay man who has been out since I was 20 years old. Never had an issue with it. Never wanted to hide it. Consider this: what if a female judge went on a singles site and put her measurements in her profile, you know, something like 36-24-36. I put my dick size on that

Manhunt profile, and I think that is what really upset the JQC. To them, it was shocking. I think that if the JQC had to focus on anything, they should have examined me to see if I had lied about the stats I put into that profile! Anyway I've gone on with my life. I'm glad I had a chance to serve. I liked doing it. It's important that we have gay judges in Florida. It's like having black judges or judges of any other groups that are being discriminated against. When I was a kid, gays were seen as criminals. When I was a young lawyer, it was like being kicked in the stomach to see court decisions that made us criminals. Being a judge was a chance to make those things right."

I concluded our breakfast by saying that something tells me that we have not seen the last chapter of his life as a lawyer. Audlin laughed and said, "Yeah, I'm not done yet. Meanwhile, I may go back to pursuing something in history and philosophy. Maybe I'll do some writing. Being a lawyer certainly beats digging holes in the hot sun. When I got accepted into USC law school, I had already done about 20 musical theater shows, and I enjoyed that. Maybe I'll do some more of that. When I look back at that mess with the JQC, I don't want to sound like a conspiracy theorist, but there were some strong feelings against marriage equality, and some harbored the belief that our right to marry would somehow pollute Christian marriages. I hope that when people look back at this time, they will say, 'You're kidding! Judge Audlin got chased off the bench because of that?' Florida is still a very divided state. When people up in Tallahassee get their hands on someone like me who is living down here in the cocoon of Key West, there is still trouble. We have a great life down here, but sometimes, I am in the pool here at Island House talking with people from all over the country and around the world. Many come from very conservative places but here they can throw off their clothes, jump in the pool, have a cocktail and do whatever they want, like kids in a candy store. I live here, so for me, there is more to life than this. Being a judge was a chance for me to do something good. Something significant. Something my lovers who have died would have been proud of. I never got all high and mighty when I put on those robes. I hope I served people well."

MARK EBENHOCH

Mark Ebenhoch is a dogged man of action. When he got it into his head that he should join the Marines, they eventually came to see things his way. When he decided to

 reconcile and sort out his personal and public lives, he forced those two stubborn sides to make peace with each other. When he decided to vanquish the private demons that wanted him dead, they threw in the towel, and he sent them packing. When Huntsman and Lee charged him with managing the public side of their battle for marriage equality, he successfully shepherded them through the perils of media scrutiny. Mark's doggedness is why Mikey Hudson, best man at Aaron Huntsman and Lee

Jones' wedding, knew he would be an excellent choice as their media contact once the couple's efforts to win marriage equality in Florida began to attract significant attention. With Mikey's urging, Aaron, who had known Mark casually and slightly for a few years as an occasional visitor to Key West, followed his own good instincts about trusting the right people. He saw the wisdom of Mikey's suggestion, and with Mark's skillful handling of all media questions and coverage, Huntsman and Jones were able to rest assured that their message would be accurately and carefully delivered.

With Mark on board, a strong team was forming, composed of unlikely players who shared a common vision for justice in Florida. On paper, Mark Ebenhoch's personal history might make you hesitate to assign him the management of the roller coaster ride that would be the fight for marriage equality in Florida, but he was up to the task.

Mark was born in Akron, Ohio in 1959 on what he calls "the lower end of the socio-economic scale" to a father who "never held a job worth a damn." Mark remembers his years of childhood as unhappy ones. He says, "I don't remember any happy times. Ours was a strange family dynamic. I don't remember any closeness. I was the second oldest child. The thing I remember most from my childhood was the death of JFK, and only because I was sent home from school to watch something on TV that I didn't understand. I was one of those kids who kept to himself. Any friends I made came and went because we used to move so often. We moved twenty-one times before I was seventeen years old. My parents just kept pulling up and moving. Arizona. California. My dad was a quote-unquote technical writer. We never owned our own home until after my parents divorced. I was eight years old then, and my Mom had to go to work doing public relations, or as a patient advocate, whatever she could get, taking whatever job women got in the early '70s. My first real memories are of Arizona, but after kindergarten, we moved to Huntington Beach, California. I went to high school in the San Fernando Valley. The first half of my schooling was in Catholic school and I hated it, but when I transferred into public high school, they were so far behind where I was, I found it boring."

Mark's mother felt that he needed a strong male influence in his life to replace his absent father. She made arrangements for him to have a "Big Brother" through the program of that name. That experience involved sex. Mark

says, " What happened with my Big Brother is something I have struggled with my whole life. I have tried to understand it and to place it. I mean I was nine years old and I spent my first weekend with this guy and the first thing he did was to take me shopping to buy a Speedo. I had to wear it to swim in his pool. All the while I was thinking like, 'What the hell is this all about?' After swimming, he made me take a shower with him. I had never been naked with anyone before. Then he wanted to wrestle on the bed. I remember he had this big wall of pictures in his kitchen of boys my age. Apparently all his little conquests. I went home and told my mother everything. That was the last time I saw him. I was told he moved away, but later I learned that my mother had reported him."

A few years later, when Mark was ten years old, he was assigned a different Big Brother. Again, sex was part of the relationship, but Mark remembers it as different from the earlier one. "We had what was eventually documented as the longest Big Brother relationship in Orange County. It went on for 27 years until his death in 1993. This guy really cared for me. I wasn't getting any love at home. I didn't feel like anyone gave a shit about me. He did, and he did more to bring me out of my shell than anyone else ever did. You could call him a true father figure or whatever. Even though he was married, when I would first sleep over his house in a basement room, he would leave his wife in his bedroom and come downstairs to my bed. Our relationship was sexual only in those early years. As I got older, and when we moved away, it changed, but when it was happening, I wasn't terrified. It was something new and different, to feel loved. I didn't mind it because he made it feel like love."

In high school, Mark threw himself wholeheartedly into shop class. Mark says, "I was hiding out in shop class. I was the king of shop class. I just barely got through all my other classes. I got a job at fifteen through a neighbor of mine. It was a stockroom job at an electronics firm in Van Nuys."

As is always the case with Mark Ebenhoch, he did not simply fulfill the basic requirements of work in the stockroom. His enthusiasm got him promoted to the purchasing department and before he had graduated from high school, he was the purchasing agent for the company. Also, while still in high school, Mark set his sights on a military career. His route into that life was not simple. He says, "I enlisted in the Marine Corps while I was still in high school. I looked down the road and figured I wasn't going to be doing anything else. I had a friend who said he wanted to be a Marine and he badgered me to go to an airshow with him. At the time, I believed what I had heard about Marines, that they ate babies and that they were real animals. I didn't want any part of them, but all the while my friend talked about them, I figured maybe I would just join the Coast Guard. So I went with him to the El Toro Marine Corps Airbase, and I was terrified but I figured that I'd be safe enough with my friend. We get to the show, and when I saw all those Harrier jets take off, I was hooked. So I go home and I tell my mother, 'I'm joining the Marines.' And she thought I had gone bonkers because I had received all kinds of scholarships for college. She signed the permission for me to enlist. Looking back on it, I guess I was an overachiever who immersed himself in anything he did. I was socially very awkward and I never did drugs or booze in high school. I returned all the scholarship funds as soon as she signed that permission to enlist.

"I had a spontaneous pneumothorax [a collapsed lung] while I was on delayed entry into boot camp. The recruiters were wondering if this would kill my chances of entering the Corps. There was a snafu, and I was waived in and went through boot camp, but just before I finished, I was yanked out! I was right at the point of graduation when they called it an erroneous enlistment. They sent me home after all that time at boot camp. I was devastated. I appealed to Senator Alan Cranston who tried to help me get back in. I immersed myself in work. For four years, I drove truck. For those four years, I was basically asexual and so afraid of the world. I was just trying to find my way.

I turned around and re-enlisted. This time everything went through. I am one of the few Marines who ever had to go through boot camp twice!

"I had an absolute ball in the Marines. Well, at least for the first half of my time in the Corps. I really thrived in that environment. I loved the structure. Everything I did worked. My rank promotions were like 'Boom!' one right after the other, but it became a love/hate relationship in the second half of my career in the Corps."

When asked about the sexual atmosphere of the Marine Corps, Mark notes that even the language of the Corps is homoerotic. He says, "There is nothing better than standing behind someone in formation and looking closely at the nape of his neck. And half of the stuff they say in the Corps is gay, like when they say, "Form up asshole to bellybutton.' It really is like being around a bunch of gay men."

Mark's good memories of his time in the Marines involve his years of active duty, including a stint in Desert Storm starting in 1991. He was with LAAD (Low Altitude Air Defense) for three months. His bad time as a Marine began in peacetime when he felt overcome by the bureaucracy of the military and with too much idle time on his hands as he transferred back and forth from active duty to Reserves.

While in the Reserves, Mark took an unusual one-time assignment that became a film career. Mark recalls, "I was in a unit in southern California at the time. Someone came in and asked the formation if anyone wanted to volunteer to work on a movie for a day. They said they would donate a thousand bucks to our baseball fund if they could get volunteers. I volunteered. That is how I met Dale Dye. At first I thought he was a jerk but as I got to know him, I respected him. He was a former Marine who had a problem with the way military movies also look fake. He wanted them to be realistic so he started a military film consulting business. He was looking for volunteers for his very first consulting gig. The movie was 'Invaders From Mars' and it would be my first picture. I said, 'Sure, I'll go fight some Martians and make it look real.' After that, I worked on the movie, 'Platoon.' I was one of about 30 to 40 real Marines in that picture. Dale chose two of us to continue working with him. Because of my connection to Dale, I could get away with all sorts of stuff. All my commanding officers knew what I was doing, but they loved it because I was training actors to give realistic performances as soldiers, and they were proud to have a Hollywood guy in their unit. So I spent those years trying to balance my being a Marine with my career being in movies. By the '90s, my worlds were colliding and I was developing some serious issues. My whole life was spinning out of control. I didn't feel there was any in-house counseling that could help me. I was dying inside while on the  outside I was experimenting with a new me. I was living three different lives at once: military, movie and personal. It was killing me and my depression kept getting worse."

Mark tried to make a lateral move into a position that he

found interesting, as an aerial navigator on a C130. This is a coveted position. In order to be considered, Mark had to give up rank in order to make the lateral transfer. He dropped from Sergeant to Corporal. As was always the case for Mark in his military career, there were obstacles to what he wanted. In this case, the flight surgeon who assessed his physical ability for the job, took a statement out of context and proclaimed him to be suffering from hay fever. Mark says, "The surgeon took a response I made to a question like, 'Do you ever sneeze?' – I had said yes, sometimes in Spring when there is a lot of pollen in the air – and used it to disqualify me. My complaint about this decision went all the way up the chain of command to the Secretary of the Navy whose office refused to counter a flight surgeon's assessment. I should have learned by then that in the Marines, you should always just give the answer they are looking for. Fuck it, you just lie if you really want something. It's not like I didn't do it on the questionnaire you had to fill out every six months to re-enlist, where it asks, 'Are you a homosexual or have you engaged in homosexual behavior?' I always checked the 'NO' box. So I spent half of my time in the Marines just trying to stay in and get something out of it."

Having gotten dropped from the program that would have led him to the position he wanted in the Marine Corps, Mark had to fight to regain the rank he forfeited to attempt the lateral move. He says, "I had commanding officers reviewing my file with disbelief. They would see my excellent service record book and see this weird pattern of repeating difficulty. I finally got my rank back – time, service, everything. I was sent to Okinawa. When I returned stateside is when my real life began. I was getting more and more pissed off with the Marines. I was sent to

North Carolina in 1993 and then DC where I trained for embassy security work. I was assigned to Paris, Ethiopia and Kenya. We were over there when Mogadishu happened. Back in North Carolina, I just decided that I had to start living my real life. DADT [Don't Ask Don't Tell] was still in force. I started stepping out. I went out to gay bars. I was having a lot of problems at the time. Living a lie was too tough for me. I hated being a third wheel when I was out with friends. I decided to get out of the military."

In Los Angeles., Mark met and fell in love with a man with whom he hoped to spend the rest of his life. The man was dying from AIDS. In the context of describing how he pursued this relationship, Mark breaks to discuss his own HIV status. "What I didn't know at the time was that I had tested positive when I came back from Okinawa. The military somehow lost my blood work. So I was positive before I started this relationship. At that time, they were looking for any way possible to dump gay people, so I do believe they really did misplace my test results because they would have used them to have me discharged. Ultimately, it was my decision to leave the military, not theirs. What with all of my evaluations saying things like, 'He is the epitome of a Marine' they wanted me to stay in the Corps. I seroconverted in '95. That was a year before the new meds came out, so the first drug I took was AZT. So I fall in love with this guy for whom I would give up everything, but he decides to pick up and move away to Portland, Oregon, to make amends with his family before he dies. The plan was that I would wind things up in California and follow him, but he cut off all communication. Through our friends, he explained that he didn't want to put me through the difficulty of his death. I tried to make it clear that I wasn't afraid of that, but he cut me out of the rest of his life. He didn't understand that one of my biggest fears was not having anybody holding my hand at the end. That was a huge fear for me since I was a kid. Thinking about him going through that was too much for me. My world fell apart. He lived about four more months. He had had a prior relationship with a guy who tossed him out because he couldn't deal with his AIDS. I had already had an experience of death from AIDS. My former Big Brother who was my friend for decades and did so much to help me died from AIDS in '93. I had to hide that from the military. I couldn't grieve. I couldn't say a thing."

In 1996, Mark tried to take his own life. Seven days of heavy drinking landed him in the hospital and close to death. In a hospital, he was informed by a doctor that his organs were shutting down and that he probably had an hour and a half left to live. Mark's mother intervened, and despite his strenuous protest – he had to be restrained – he was moved to a VA hospital. He embarked on a long and bumpy – there were a few other attempts at suicide – road to recovery through therapy. Mark says, " The VA saved my life. Those doctors finally realized that I had been misdiagnosed. I am actually bipolar but I don't present that way. A San Francisco doctor saw my case come through and said he wanted it. He put me on a specific medication that changed my life like night and day. My mother had some mental illness issues so she understood my problems. So I got through it. I learned that you have to find the right medication. I also learned that my depression is the kind that goes through cycles, when I feel a bad time coming on, the first thing I do is make a call to say that I am in trouble. That is the hard lesson, learning to own your psychological reality and not to let it destroy you. I learned that all the fighting I felt I had to do in my life comes from anger that wells up. I expressed my cycles of depression through anger. Now when I feel bad, I let everyone know to either leave me alone or give me lots of lovin' and huggin'!"

Mark ended his military career in 2000 when he retired from the Reserves.

In San Francisco, celebrating his 45th birthday with friends, Mark made a spontaneous decision. He remembers, "I looked at my friends and announced, 'I'm selling my house and I'm moving to Florida.' I didn't need to live in a big city because I had already done that. I looked at the map of Florida and skipped over Miami. I also didn't want the redneck parts of Florida. I picked Cape Coral thinking it would be perfect. I hated it there and moved to St Petersburg after a year. Three and a half years ago, I bought a house in Key West, and I moved into it full time about a year ago. I had fallen in love with Key West as a visitor. It was kooky and crazy and full of nuts just like me, and there were gay ones too! No one cares if you're gay or straight in this town. I have some straight conservative neighbors who, if you lived next to them in Alabama, would slit your throat, but down here, they are friends with every drag queen  in town because that's what they have come to know. Key West is all of my worlds combined. There is that to love, plus the weather.

"My first visit was in '08. That is when I met Aaron. He was working at the bar at Bourbon Street Pub. He was so sweet and talkative. We didn't really become friends. He was just someone I always saw when I dropped into Key West. Meanwhile, I had started to become an activist over the Prop 8 issue, and in Florida I had organized protests over Amendment 2. When my friend Mikey Hudson called me with the news that the marriage ban in Florida had been overturned, I was shocked. He said they were having a victory party at Aqua that night and he wanted me to come and meet the guys who did it. When Mikey introduced me to Aaron and Lee that night, I said, 'Oh you're *that* Aaron!' I was wearing an Absolut promotional tee shirt with a rainbow flag on it, and Aaron points at it and says, 'I gave you that shirt years ago!' Mikey then told Aaron and Lee that I could help them. They were being inundated with media inquiries. Mikey figured I could handle all that because of my Hollywood experience. Aaron wanted to know more about me. He has this uncanny ability to look at someone and know that he can trust him. Sometimes he is a little too trusting. We are alike in that way. So Aaron calls me at home and says, 'Will you do this for us?' and I said, 'When do you want to meet?' and he says, 'Now!' It was my Marine Corps training that help me hit the ground running. Aaron told his lawyer Bernadette, 'We have a media guy" and she says, 'Who is this guy?'"

In the course of handling media for Huntsman and Jones, Bernadette Restivo's question would be often repeated by others, but no one ever asks it twice. Within minutes of meeting with Huntsman, Jones, Restivo, Hudson and Mark Ebenhock, you understand why they are a success and you never again question the skills of the dogged Marine.

SUSAN KENT

Susan Kent has always known exactly who she is, a crusader against injustice large or small. She says her mother remembers when she came rushing home from third grade agitated about the fact that a classmate had been wrongly punished by their teacher for something he did not do. Susan says, "I was carrying on about this, and finally my mother asked me how I was involved in the situation and I told her I wasn't. I said, 'But it's wrong. It doesn't matter if I am not the one who got punished. It's just wrong, Mommy!'" Susan cannot help herself. She cannot resist fighting for an underdog or railing against an injustice. Of course she said yes when Aaron Huntsman asked her to be part of their little band of Key West hobbits who were going to leave the Shire in order to do battle with the monstrous and unjust powers put in play by Anita Bryant.

Susan was born in Ohio and started life in a suburb of Cleveland. Her family moved to South Carolina while she was a child and that is where she went to college, majoring in English. She has lived in Key West for twenty-four years, longer than she has lived anywhere else. This makes her a

"Freshwater Conch" in the truest sense. She is, however, one of the very few people who moved to Key West with a job already in hand. Most folks come for vacation, fall in love with it, make the move and then think about what they will do for work. She says, "I had been working for a regional airline carrier for several years when they transferred me to Key West. I had that job until February of 1998 when I was summarily dismissed. Why? American Airlines was one of the first airlines to develop a gay and lesbian marketing department. They hired a really sharp guy to go after the pink dollar. They did this because they had gotten some extremely bad press about two separate incidents that had the gay community threatening to boycott the airline. The first one happened at the end of the March on Washington in 1993. It involved one of the planes returning to Dallas from DC. An American Airlines employee wrote a very nasty email warning the staff in Dallas that when the plane touched down, they should carefully sterilize all the silverware that had been on that flight because it had so many gay passengers. The message was implying that those passengers were all carrying AIDS which they thought could be spread by the silverware. The second incident involved an ACT UP member who had devised an action in which he got on a flight, produced an IV kit and proceeded to try to set up an IV drip on the plane. Obviously that is not a medical procedure that could be accommodated on the spot by the staff, and was not allowed at the time. They told him he couldn't do it. He said that he would not get off the plane unless they had him arrested, which they did. He claimed he was being arrested because of his HIV. The press was horrible for American Airlines and so they formed a gay and lesbian marketing department. Many large companies started encouraging diversity groups for their employees, including

LGBT groups. When the LGBT diversity group formed, I jumped in with both feet. I had been an activist since college. I began working for gay rights while I was in college. I went to Winthrop College – now Winthrop University. It had been a women's college but had gone coed the year before I was a freshman. The ratio of women to men was still about ten to one, so, as you can imagine, there was a strong lesbian culture there. These

days it's a typical state college with a typical demographic but when I started there in 1977, I was warned to look out for the Phys Ed majors because they were supposedly all lesbians. I said, 'Really? Where's the Phys Ed department?' I was an English major but I had no problem finding my way to the gym if I had to. My first real 'out' activism was in a psychology class. Our professor invited each of us to 'teach' a chapter in our textbook. Naturally, I jumped on the 'Alternative Lifestyles' chapter. Along with another classmate, I rounded up a few friends and we walked into the class, sat down in front, and I said, 'I'm a lesbian. These are my gay friends. What do you want to know?' It was probably my first publically 'out' action. Since then, I have never stopped taking about the fact that I am gay. Even if I answer a telemarketing sales call, I always work it into the conversation in the first two minutes."

Susan returns with a shrug to the subject of having been fired from the airlines on what seemed like trumped up charges of cash mishandling. She admits she did not always follow protocol but that neither did the other managers because of staff limitations and the press of time. Her regional manager was not too keen on the new gay and lesbian employee group and did not like Susan's very vocal and energetic participation in it. She had also confronted the regional carrier's president during an employee tabletop discussion, asking him to respond to the position paper proposing domestic partner benefits that had been put forward by their group. She thinks the charges against her were invented because of her strong participation in the group. Eventually, her dismissal was made non-specific and was credited to the elimination of her position.

In addition to working for the United Way, Susan has been on the board of directors of the Key West Business Guild and she was also the president of the Key West Gay And Lesbian Community Center (GLCC.) Through that position, she was given responsibility for the project that brought Aaron to Key West when he first met Lee. Susan recalls, "When I was president of the GLCC, we finally secured funding for the '25Rainbow Sea-To-Sea Gay Flag' project. [To celebrate the 25th anniversary of the creation of his gay flag, Gilbert Baker made a 1.25 mile-long eight-color flag that was stretched on June 15, 2003, the entire length of Duval Street connecting the Atlantic Ocean to the Gulf Coast Sea.] We put together a plan to get the flag unfurled for our Gay Pride event. That is when I first met Gilbert Baker. On that project, my co-chairs were Tom Wheaton who owns Paradise Health and Fitness, and Heather Carruthers who is now our county mayor. The project was huge, and Aaron was hired by Absolut Vodka, one of our major sponsors. They gave us more than a quarter of a million dollars and Aaron was brought down from Fort Lauderdale to promote the brand. We were expecting to have about three thousand volunteers and Absolut provided us with a tee shirt for everyone who touched the flag. Aaron had contacts because he was a bartender in Fort Lauderdale. That is how we all met, but over the years, we never really were close until Facebook became popular. Aaron would post a photo of the flag and I would see it and start tagging people in it. We reconnected that way. Aaron said that he noticed I had event planning and marketing experience, and he wondered if I could help him. They had already filed their case with Monroe County. I immediately said yes and volunteered to help with social media. I created pages for him and wrote press releases and set up events and fundraisers to try to bring in a few dollars to cover expenses such as travel. Bernadette and her legal team were working pro bono but there were other expenses that Aaron and Lee had no way to cover. Then Mark Ebenhoch joined the team and he was a powerhouse for getting media attention. I felt really lucky to play a part on that team. I didn't have a huge part, but I was able to help bring awareness to what Aaron and Lee were doing. I traveled with them to DC for the Supreme Court hearings.

"In DC, I remember talking with Aaron and Lee and Mark about how I had wanted marriage equality for decades even when it wasn't popular in the gay community. I was focused more on the legal benefits, and the tax and financial benefits, but, as we know, what was needed was a strategy that would change the hearts and minds of Americans by showing them how we love each other. Hearing about equal rights to a Social Security inheritance wasn't going to win the battle. People were so naïve about the situation of gay people and said some strange things when marriage equality became law. People said to me, 'Are you going to get married to get benefits now?' and I would say, 'No. You can't marry someone who is deceased and then retroactively get benefits. You need to marry someone while they are alive!"

Susan is referring to the fact that her partner Teri whom she calls "wife" even though they never legally married had died in December of 2010. When Susan tells the story of their seventeen years together, she speaks with deep gratitude for the support and honor that both their families gave them despite the lack of legal protections.

"Teri had raised a family and had come out in her 40s. She had been married and divorced five times which we thought was hilarious because all five of them put together didn't equal the same number of years that she and I had together. I met her in Key West in 1993. I had been living here for a couple of years. She had just been coming here on vacation for several years. She and her partner at the time decided to move here. They got into town and within two weeks her partner dumped her! This was good timing for me! I was living with someone in some kind of relationship which had been ending for a while, so when we met, there was an immediate attraction. We actually tried to talk about it like adults and said, 'Well, when we get everything else cleared up we'll see each other', but of course we didn't wait. We made our own private commitment to each other on Christmas Day, 1993, and moved in together within a few months. Of course all of our friends said it wouldn't last because we were both coming out of other relationships, but it did last obviously. We had been together exactly a year and a half when we had our public commitment ceremony with Steve Torrence our dear friend who is the pastor and minister of the MCC church marrying us. He also married Aaron and Lee. Years later, when marriage equality started happening in places around the world, we had friends who were going to Spain for it. Teri and I

talked it over and we both agreed that when we came home from Spain we still wouldn't be really married. Even when it became legal in Massachusetts and we thought about it again, we still didn't want to come back to Florida and still be not married. We kept hoping it was going to happen in Florida because we wanted to have a legal wedding in our town and in our state. Then when it became legal in California, we decided to get married there, because we traveled to California every year. That is where Teri was from. Her family, kids and grandkids were there, so it felt like home. By the time our trip came around, Prop 8 had passed and it was no longer legal there, so we never did get married. Teri died in December of 2010 and I remember thinking that maybe we should have done what so many of our friends did who gave up on waiting for marriage to come to Florida. Maybe we should have gone out of state for it. Some people say it's just a piece of paper, but not having it made us feel like second-class citizens.

"Teri and I felt the same way about adoption which we had

considered. She was fifteen years older than I. She had raised her children and by the time gay adoption became legal, it was pretty much out of the question for us."

Susan always wanted to have a child. Whether or not she actually bore the child was not important to her. She simply wanted to raise a child and to form a family. She says, "I tried getting pregnant via a sperm donor. Teri and I felt that it would be better to know the donor. We wanted to have full parental rights but we wanted to have someone who could choose to have a role in the child's life without legal or financial obligations. We chose our close friend Jean-Claude Gosselin who was well known in Key West. He was the king of Fantasy Fest one year. He was family to us, and we spent every Thanksgiving and Christmas and all of our holidays together. He was interested in having a child but not actually raising one, which was perfect for us. We had many sessions trying to get the magic juice from Jean-Claude whenever it was ovulation time for me. We weren't doing in vitro fertilization because we didn't have tons of money and our insurance wasn't covering it, so my doctor was kind enough to provide us with some tubing. We didn't exactly use a turkey baster but it was pretty close to it. Jean-Claude would visit the house, make a donation, and we would do our thing and wait for the results. Suddenly he stopped answering our calls and then he was making excuses for not coming over, and finally when we bumped into him, he took us aside in tears and said 'I've just tested positive.' Our main concern was about him. We knew that there were processes in place for washing the sperm and making it safe but we didn't do all that. It just wasn't meant to be. For the rest of his life, Jean-Claude and I called each other mommy and daddy, and sometimes we'd say things like, 'Imagine. If we had done it, he'd be six years old now. A first-grader!'"

Susan thinks it is probably a good thing that they did not have a child or adopt one because all of her attention had to be focused on Teri when she became sick. She says, "I guess everything turned out the way it was supposed to. Teri was breathing a sigh of relief because she had already taken her turn in parenting and she wasn't going to have to do it again. I love my father and he has always loved me and been supportive but sometimes he just knocks me over with the crazy questions he asks or things he supposes. He makes me realize how other people around us see gay people. When I told him that if gay adoption had been legal, he'd have had another grandchild, he was amazed that it wasn't legal. It was the same when the idea for starting the gay and lesbian community center down here was suggested. People said, 'What for? You people already have everything you want down here.' Like my father, they didn't know anything about lack of protections for employment, housing, health and adoption or marriage rights. They only know about wealthy people like Rosie O'Donnell who could afford to go out of state to adopt the kids she wanted and then come back to Florida with them.

"It was good that Teri and I had gotten every kind of legally protective document imaginable when we made our commitment to each other. Power of attorney, medical powers, durable powers. We never traveled without those pieces of paper because in an emergency there might be no way for strangers to understand or respect our relationship. When Teri was in the hospital dying and was placed in hospice care, two of her children were here with us to the very end. They were very supportive of our relationship. I remember a meeting we all had with the hospice care-giver.

Teri's son asked if they could put her in a bigger bed. The care-giver looked at him confused because Teri was down to maybe 80 pounds. I knew the care-giver — this is Key West where we all know each other — and I explained that he was asking for me because every night I would get into that bed with my wife to comfort her. Teri's kids could see that this gave her peace. I was in that bed when Teri breathed her last breath. I had fallen asleep and her daughter was holding her hand and then they woke me up. There was so much paperwork to be signed. Teri had had time to make decisions about her memorial service and she had decided to donate her body for medical research. She had an autoimmune disease that was very rare so she was happy to do that. She died at 3AM and we had to wait for the funeral home in Key Largo that was handling the donation to arrive. I was being asked to sign off on the release of her remains, and I turned to Teri's daughter and said, 'I have no rights here. You are the next of kin. All of our legal protections expired the moment she died. By law, I am just a stranger.' Her kids were so wonderful to me. They looked at me and said, 'That's not right. For seventeen years you have been with her and taken care of her. You are her wife.' They honored all of Teri's wishes. I am still close to them. With Teri's great-grandchild, I am called Grandma Sue. I guess I finally got the family I wanted but I never thought I'd be a great-grandmother at 52!

"And then when I went home to visit my father and mother shortly after Teri died, my father again said something that floored me. He said, 'Well now that she's gone, and it's too late for you, at least you can stop working for gay marriage.' I had to explain to him that it was never just about me. Even though my wife was dead, I still wanted everyone to have the right to get married. That is when my mother came into the room and she heard this conversation and she just laughed and said to my father, 'Of course she isn't going to stop. She came out of my womb kicking and screaming 'It's not fair! It's not fair! It's not fair!'"

MIKEY HUDSON

Best Man at the marriage of Aaron Huntsman and Lee Jones, MiKey Hudson is the kind of scrappy little guy you should want on your side in a fight. MiKey spells his name with a capital "K" to indicate proudly his Conch status as a longtime Key West resident. He waves away the distinction between Freshwater and Saltwater Conchs, saying, "I'm a Conch and I always will be."

Hudson is originally from Poplar Point, Maryland where he survived both Catholic and public schooling and the bullying that came his way not because he was perceived as gay but because he was short. He says, "I knew I was gay when I was seven years-old. I wasn't into dolls, but I did like playing with the dollhouse we had at school. It's funny that, when I grew up, I didn't get the gay decorating gene. I must have lost it somewhere. My big problem as a kid wasn't getting beat up, but I had a birth defect that kept me out of a lot of physical stuff. I had bladder and kidney infections until I was sixteen, and I had to take 54 pills a day through high school. Even though I knew what I wanted, sex didn't happen until I was sixteen and got a job and a car. Right away, I made the mistake of getting picked up by the county queer and sure enough someone saw my car parked where it shouldn't have been and I got caught. My mother wanted me to be institutionalized. My father talked her out of that and said to me, 'You're my son and I will always love you.' So they sent me to a psychologist. After awhile, my mother asked him, 'Is he fixed yet?' and he told her that I was a very well-adjusted gay man. My mother didn't speak with me for about a year after that, but  she came around. All this trouble took me out of school from tenth grade on, but later I got my GED."

MiKey moved to Key West in 1993 after having visited many times. He says, "Remember the summer of '92? It's the summer that never was because of the crazy weather. I was here for it and when I went back to Maryland, I told my mother that I was moving, and I turned around and came back for good. I was 34 years old. I am on disability, so I do a lot of volunteer work down here, helping the HIV/AIDS community. I have been HIV+ for 26 years."

MiKey met Aaron Huntsman when they were both working on the *25Rainbow Sea to Sea Project*. [In 2003, a two kilometer (1.3 mile) version of Gilbert Baker's original eight-color gay flag was unfurled down the length of Duval Street, connecting the Atlantic Ocean and the Gulf Coast Sea, marking the 25th anniversary of the flag. Sections of that flag were distributed worldwide.] He says that he and Aaron had often spoken of marriage equality and hoped that Key West would lead Florida in overturning the ban.

When asked about how his group of friends hatched the plan to demand marriage equality, MiKey's recollection of the facts is blurry. The days leading up to the denial of a marriage license, the filing of the *Huntsman v. Heavilin* case, the judgment, the stay, the appeal, the final ruling and the marriage of Aaron and Lee constitute a wonderful memory for him, the details of which may be slightly fuzzy, but the personal importance of what unfolded comes through clearly in his voice as he tries to outline the story.

"The bridge between [Attorney] Bernadette [Restivo] and Aaron and Lee was a lawyer who had been affiliated with Bernadette's practice at one time. Bernadette was hesitant about taking on Aaron and Lee as clients but her law partner at the time, Jessica Reilly, was in favor of it and Bernadette soon was on board. We all had this idea that Key West really was where gay Florida history had always been made. The rest of Florida gave us Anita Bryant, thanks. For example, I had a boyfriend here who was big in the Jaycees, and we were one of the first gay couples recognized nationally in the Jaycees, so I had this feeling that Key West should always be first in changing things. Now I'm 56 and I think back on my early time here before there were three Starbucks here and a CVS on every corner and I miss that old wild Key West. Maybe it's just because I'm older and I've been single for seven years and everything has changed, but Aaron and I wanted to do what real Conchs do when there is injustice. We don't stay quiet.

"Now I have to warn you that I'm not going to sugarcoat this when I talk about the days just before April 1, 2014 when we went to the courthouse to get the license. I'll preface this by saying that Equality Florida has its place, but should they take $240,000 in donations from Key West snowbirds who don't know where their money is really going and think it stays in Key West? Anyway, Aaron and Lee put out the word that they were looking for other Key West couples to go with them to the courthouse to try to get marriage licenses. Some couples said they wanted to, but finally, Aaron and Lee knew they would have to do this on their own. Now I had never met anyone with Equality Florida but somehow I think they got word of what we had planned, and that we here in Monroe County would be the first to do this in Florida. Suddenly we are getting frantic calls with information that Equality Florida is going to send down some couples of their own on April 11 to go to the courthouse. We had planned to go on April 7. We knew we had to move fast. Tom was on the phone with Bernadette about when we should pull the trigger, and I'm looking at the calendar and I suggested April 1. Lee didn't much like that idea because it would make it seem like an April Fool's Day joke, but Aaron and I thought it was an awesome idea and so we all settled on that date.

"Max [Max Watson who was at the time a co-worker with Aaron at Aqua Nightclub] went to the courthouse very early that day to make sure they were open and to make sure none of the Equality Florida couples had gotten there before us. Aaron, Lee and I met at Tom's house. Kenne' [Key West blogger Kenneth J. Tucker, jr] came too. When we got to the courthouse, Kenne' started the camera and made a recording of the whole thing. Aaron and Lee walked up to the counter and asked the lady for a marriage license. She said she was sorry but couldn't oblige them. Then she handed them that disgusting piece of paper, the denial slip. She wanted them to sign it. Aaron and Lee refused. She then called Ron Saunders who is the council for the county Clerk. Ron came out and greeted us – you have to remember that in Key West everybody knows everybody - and apologized and said that is the way the law is. We weren't thirty seconds out the door of that office when Aaron phoned Bernadette who immediately filed the suit.

"At that time I had never even met Bernadette, and Aaron and Lee had met her only once. She came down to Key West to meet us all at 801 Bourbon where Lee works. She walks in the door and says, 'Hi. I'm Bernie. I really need to pee. Where's the bathroom.' We loved her right off!

"I think that's when I started saying 'We got this!' I said that over and over when the case was going on. Aaron and Lee got tired of hearing it and used to tell me to shut up, but I just knew our 'Love Is Love Key West' campaign would win. I never had a doubt."

Aaron and MiKey had checked with folks in California who had originated the *"LoveIsLove"* slogan and they received permission to use it in Key West. Their friend Susan Kent formulated the *"LoveIsLoveKeyWest"* campaign without any corporate sponsors. MiKey thinks this is another fine example of how they worked independently and without relying on groups like Equality Florida. He says, "We didn't answer to anyone. We were not scripted by anyone. We generated and managed all the media attention that came our way."

MiKey describes a meet-and-greet event held upstairs at 801 Bourbon in mid-June of 2014. The purpose of the event was to solicit help to defray the expenses assumed by Bernadette Restivo's law firm. He says, "We had a guest registry and a box for donations. When we arrived, we saw that Equality Florida had taken over the tables at the top of the stairs and that they were asking people for a $25 donation. I took care of that right away. I told them I didn't think it was right for them to ask our guests for $25 and I told them to move their stuff. Which they did."

MiKey also remembers the excitement of attending the hearing on July 7, 2014 at the courthouse on Plantation Key at Mile Marker 88. The Key West contingent had to start their drive at dawn if they wanted to arrive on time and get into the courtroom. Ever the mischief-maker, MiKey told Equality Florida's Key West development director that there would be 300 allies and protestors lining the road to the courthouse and filling the few seats of its small courtroom. This fabrication alarmed Equality Florida, and their representative arrived with placards and handouts to counter the imaginary protest. MiKey remembers Equality Florida's person walking up and down the aisles of the courtroom lecturing the attendees about how to behave and react to protestors and to the presentation to be made by Attorney Mathew Staver of the liberty Counsel who would speak against marriage equality. MiKey says, "My answer was, 'Look, we have lived with this stuff all our lives. We know how to handle this. Also, Aaron and I had started a rumor that Judge Garcia was going to rule from the bench. Why? Just for fun, and to poke the bear, Equality Florida. They hadn't been paying much attention to us so we had to create our own news sometimes. We wanted to be part of a team but it felt like we were being excluded. We did things to get noticed not because we wanted to pick a fight but because Aaron and Lee were the face of marriage equality in Florida and people needed to see that.

"Bernadette was asking Judge Garcia when he would issue a ruling, and he was saying, 'Soon,' but we knew he had taken an entire month off just to read the cases he took on when David Audlin resigned, so we figured we would have to wait awhile for the ruling.

"On July 16, Aaron and I went to an Equality Florida event at a bar on Duval Street in Key West called Wine-O. We

wore our *LoveIsLove* tee shirts and when we walked in the door, someone from Equality Florida comes up to us and says 'You're a little underdressed.' We didn't care. And then, when the same person asked Aaron to get her a glass of wine because he is a bartender – it was her idea of a joke – we didn't care.

"That was the evening before I got the call from Bernadette saying we had won. She couldn't get a hold of Aaron who was involved in a meeting that he didn't want interrupted. I got to Lee and told him that he needed to get dressed and get with Aaron right away. You need to remember that these guys are bartenders who work nights and this is morning when they usually sleep. Suddenly everything is crazy with us trying to get in one place with our *LoveIsLove* tee shirts and the media wants comments, and I called Mark [Ebenhoch] and told him to get down here right away, and the head of *Equality Florida*, Nadine Smith, is calling up Aaron to congratulate him, and we somehow all get to 801 Bourbon with our shirts on, and in comes Doug Mayberry who is with *Equality Florida*, and he hands Aaron and Lee a script, so they will know what to say to the media. And they hand it back to him and say 'No thanks. We will take advice from our attorney, Bernadette Restivo.' They didn't need any script. They spoke from the heart.

"Everything broke loose after that. Even though *Equality Florida* made the point that our ruling applied only to Monroe County which is just one of 67 Florida counties, out hotels were immediately swamped with calls to book weddings. TV stations are sending crews down from Miami to cover all this in time to get it on the evening news. Aaron had the idea that we should  do a rally the next day to encourage Judge Garcia to lift his stay on the ruling. That is when Mark stepped in and began to be our point person with the media. He did more with just his cell phone and a laptop than any public relations firm with a huge staff could have done.

"Then, on July 25, Judge Sable ruled the same way in Miami, and all the cases were merged and the Federal Judge Hinkle also ruled the same way, and we had Attorney General Pam Bondi appealing all these decisions and asking that the stay not be lifted. So we are waiting to see what would happen with the appeal, and I said to Aaron and Lee, 'You guys are gonna be on view everywhere in the world so we better get our nails done. We were at Headlines Salon on Duval Street getting manicures and talking about how Aaron and Lee should be the first to get married after the stay is lifted, when we got the news. I think Judge Garcia lifted the stay at 1PM and Judge Sable lifted hers at 2PM.

MiKey gets emotional when asked to summarize how he felt standing next to Aaron and Lee at their wedding. "I looked out at the cheering crowd and the TV crews. I thought about how we had been told that we were not media ready. That wasn't true. We were ready to celebrate this beautiful wedding. It was jubilant and wonderful. I thought about Mat Staver's comments at the hearing and all the nonsense that comes out of the religious right. He got served up on a Conch platter by our straight Catholic woman lawyer! I thought about all the generations to come who will never know a day when they could not get married. It was the proudest moment of my life."

TONY CICALESE AND BRIAN STEELE

Tony Cicalese and Brian Steele, both 44 years old and living in Oakland Park, Florida, have been together for ten years, and more or less married, coupled, joined, committed, partnered or you pick the word for nine years. Their road to the altar(s) involved a strange twist in the Florida fight for marriage equality that had them dropped as plaintiffs in the *Huntsman v Heavilin* Monroe County case that became the first Florida suit to win in court. Are they bitter about that? Hardly.

Cicalese, owner of *We Got The Beats* record store on Federal Highway just north of Commercial Boulevard, and Steele who is in management in the food service industry, are both karaoke fiends. The men say that the friends you do karaoke with are almost always "sisters" rather than lovers, so their mutual attraction surprised them. Also, Cicalese, a bartender at Boom when they first met, resisted the possibility that Steele could become a boyfriend, saying, "I was telling anyone who would listen that I was on a serious break from romance and that I was absolutely not interested in anyone for a relationship. After a few weeks with Brian, my coworkers were doing an imitation of me saying 'Hi, I'm Tony Cicalese and this is my not-a-boyfriend Brian.'"

On September 9, 2007, they entered into a civil union in New Jersey. The ceremony was attended by supportive relatives from both sides. Cicalese and Steele still consider this to be the day they became married, even though it was not legally or literally a marriage.

When marriage equality became law in California, Cicalese spotted an $11 Spirit airfare to Los Angeles. He says, "I called Brian and told him to drop everything. We flew out there, got married by a Justice of the Peace with two friends I had from a gay rights chat room as our witnesses. We went to Disneyland for our second honeymoon."

Gay bartenders all know each other, and because Aaron Huntsman had been a bartender at Cathode Ray in Fort Lauderdale when Cicalese was tending bar at Alibi, they were friends. Cicalese began to follow Huntsman's Facebook posts about his plans to file a marriage equality suit in Monroe County. He says, "When I saw what Aaron was doing, it went straight to my heart. This is what I myself always wanted to do, have our marriage recognized by Florida. I didn't think we could afford a lawyer to help us do that. When I left some supportive comments on Aaron's posts, he contacted me, asking if we would be interested in being part of their case by joining the suit. Of course we said yes."

A conversation with Huntman's Attorney Bernadette Restivo and a quick trip to the law offices of Attorney Dean Trantalis to have notarized the documents adding them to what would become the landmark *Huntsman v*

Heavilin case were all that was needed for Cicalese and Steele to become part of Florida gay rights history. Cicalese says, "Aaron and Bernadette were saying 'The more the merrier! We can use another couple.' They described their strategy and their plans to raise funds for the expenses to come. Brian and I knew we would be a good addition to their suit even though we were not wealthy because we were a solid and very traditional type of couple. We began to hear that there was some blow back from Equality Florida about Aaron's initiative, and we knew that Bernadette was trying her best to structure her suit in a cooperative way with what Equality Florida was doing elsewhere. We were told that Equality Florida advised Bernadette to take us off the suit because we were already married in another state, and that if a married couple was part of the suit it would leave it open to the possibility of appeal. So, we had to go back and get our names legally removed from the suit."

Cicalese and Steele admit that they may have not understood correctly the strategic reasons for their being dropped from *Huntsman v Heavilin* but they accepted the premise that their exit would help the case win. What followed, however, is important because it demonstrates the true valor and dedication of the two couples involved, Cicalese/Steele and Huntsman/Jones. Cicalese says, "Aaron went out of his way to keep us informed and involved in the suit. When it came time for the hearing, Brian and I booked a hotel room in Islamorada for the night before the court date. We shared that room with Aaron, Lee, their eventual best man MiKey Hudson, a photographer and our dog. During the hearing, Brian and I were in the front row of the courtroom. It felt great to be there, but two weeks later when I read Judge Garcia's decision, I was very disappointed to read that the decision would not apply to couples married out of state. All I could think was that we had been right there in the front row. If we had been part of the suit, maybe we would have been part of the victory."

With their California marriage made valid and recognized at home because of the Supreme Court decision that followed, Cicalese decided to surprise his husband with a private renewal-of-vows ceremony. When Steele arrived home from work, Cicalese led him into their backyard which he had decorated and where a clergyman friend Joel Slotnick awaited them. Cicalese promised Steele that this would be the very last time he would ever marry him. They say third time's the charm.

EPILOGUE
THE SACRED CLOTH

It is good to know that Aaron Huntsman and Lee Jones were victorious in their demand for marriage equality. They are happily married and their union is recognized and celebrated not just in Key West but in all of Florida, in all the United States and in many other countries.

Unfortunately, the legacy of Anita Bryant is not entirely vanquished. It thrives in the many anti-gay Christian religions that condemn or shun LGBT people. It lurks in the offices of public clerks who still refuse to process same-sex marriage licenses by calling their homophobia religious freedom. It howls in the voices of politicians who pander to bigots by creating unfounded fears and concerns for the safety of children in public restrooms, and it slaughters us when it fills the deranged with enough misguided anger to walk into a gay nightclub in Orlando and murder 49 innocent people.

Aaron and Lee met because of the Sea-to-Sea Rainbow Flag project in Key West. To celebrate the 25th anniversary of the creation of his flag, Gilbert Baker made a 1.25 mile eight-color gay rainbow flag that was stretched the length of Duval Street on June 15, 2003, connecting the Atlantic Ocean to the Gulf Coast Sea. Aaron was brought in from Fort Lauderdale by Absolut Vodka to work on this project. That is when he met Lee. That is also when he met Susan Kent who, as president of Key West Gay And Lesbian Community Center, coordinated the project.

Mark Ebenhoch is the custodian of Section 93 of the Sea-to-Sea flag which was divided into 250 sections, some 25' long and some 100' long. Many of the sections were donated and sent to cities worldwide. Ebenhoch says, "Over the last 12 years sections have been featured at celebrations in Manchester, England; Vancouver, Toronto and Stockholm, in addition to many major cities in states across America. Also, one was displayed at the 2010 winter Olympics in Vancouver, and one was carried by *Equality Virginia* in the 2014 inauguration Parade for Governor Terry McAuliffe."

Some sections are held in reserve and are stored in New York. Key West kept one 100' section and two 25' sections, one of which is Section 93, now a well traveled, slightly tattered and potent symbol of LGBT victories and ongoing struggles. Ebenhoch is the founder and president of *The Sacred Cloth Project*.

Stephen Sunday, a close friend of Aaron and Lee, who had been crowned king of Key West's annual *Fantasy Fest* in 2014, talks about how Section 93 got to the steps of the Supreme Court. He says, "Section 93 came back to life because of a conversation I had with Aaron and Lee when they invited me to accompany them to DC for the Supreme court hearing of the Obergefell case. We wanted to bring something that would visually represent us as being from Key West. I had the idea that taking the flag with us would have the biggest impact. Aaron loved the idea and called Stephen K. Murray-Smith who is responsible for the flag. Steve gave his permission but said that Section 93 was not in good condition and needed some repair work. Aaron called Sushi [Key West's world-famous drag queen who is annually lowered in a gigantic high heeled shoe during the New Year's Eve countdown] asking if she could do the needed sewing. Sushi became our own Key West Betsey Ross! After getting back from Washington DC, I handed off the torch of Section 93 to Mark Ebenhoch who has given it more honor than could ever be written. I was the little torch that brought life back to section 93 and Mark is the bigger torch that continues to keep burning for The Sacred Cloth."

Section 93 hung from the rooftop of the DC home of Dan Bready and Kevin Dickinson when they hosted the Key West plaintiffs during the *Obergefell v. Hodges* hearings. It was also unfurled on the steps of the Supreme Court during those hearings. That is when the plaintiffs who were gathered there from around the country first began to refer to it as "The Sacred Cloth."

The Louisiana Federal 5th Circuit Plaintiffs, Derek and Jon Penton-Robicheaux, reached out to Ebenhoch, requesting that Section 93 accompany them and the Grand Marshals of the 44th Southern Decadence Parade in New Orleans in September, 2015. It was carried by plaintiffs from Louisiana, Key West and Alabama.

Kentucky couple Timothy Love and Lawrence Ysunza, the last of the Obergefell plaintiffs to wed, were looking to adorn their church with banners, signs or memorabilia from their national fight for marriage equality. Ebenhoch sent them Section 93. Before it left Key West, the mayor and a group of well-wishers gathered for a send-off photo as a surprise gift from Key West to the couple. While it was in Louisville, all six couples in the *Bourke v. Beshear* suit which had been combined with *Obergefell* were photographed with Section 93 at the wedding.

While in Kentucky, Section 93 was unfurled at the office of infamous County Clerk Kim Davis who had defied the Supreme Court by refusing to issue marriage licenses to same-sex couples.

Its name is significant. Churches are places of sacred objects and rituals. Many LGBT people who proclaim their sexuality are deprived of the ability to participate in the sacredness of their own beliefs. Driven out of the churches of their upbringing, they are forced to invent new rituals and new symbols for what they hold sacred.

The sight of Aaron, Lee and their friends boldly stretching the billowing 25 foot Section 93 above the steps of the Supreme Court brought many folks to tears. I remember watching a group of young school children brought by their wise teacher to witness this important moment in American history as they ran, played and sang beneath the benevolent tent of Section 93 glowing in the full sun of that radiant day. Some of those children may grow up to be gay. They will remember that day, and they will revere The Sacred Cloth long after those who held it above them are gone.

Ebenhoch also seems to have instinctively understood the healing power of The Sacred Cloth. All religions use their sacred objects, images, verses and music to overcome sadness, to express grief or to cope with tragedy. For this reason, he brought Section 93 to Orlando where it became a powerful symbol of survival and hope in the days following the massacre.

Ebenhoch also brought Section 93 to Sydney, Australia for the Sydney Gay and Lesbian Mardi Gras Parade on March 5, 2016. It was carried by the United States Embassy delegation led by the first openly gay US ambassador to a G20 nation, Ambassador John Berry. Marching by his side was French Ambassador Christophe Lecoutrie with the staff of the French Embassy. Before leaving Australia, Ebenhoch performed and documented a ceremonial dip of Section 93 into the South Pacific Ocean making it a hemisphere-to-hemisphere flag.

Ebenhoch's objective is to have The Sacred Cloth be acquired by the Smithsonian. He says, "The folks at the Smithsonian do not yet understand the significance of the sacred cloth. They seem to think that it is just another rainbow flag. The process leading to their recognition of its significance has been difficult but worth the work. Meanwhile, I continue to bring it wherever healing is needed. Rowan County in Kentucky wants it for their first ever Pride celebration as a symbol of triumph over their county clerk, Kim Davis."

Ebenhoch wants to bring the Sacred Cloth across the 90 miles that separate Key West from Cuba. He says, "It's been all over the world and now I would love to have Section 93 make the short but significant leap from Key West to Cuba to cheer the LGBT community of Cuba as they enjoy new freedom."

The victory of Aaron Huntsman and Lee Jones continues to bear fruit in the lives of LGBT communities worldwide. Anita Bryant is still with us in flesh and in spirit. She may not wish to talk about her history with the LGBT community, but her silence is loud. Victories like that of Aaron and Lee will make her actions against us a small and odd footnote in the full history of LGBT equality.

TEXT OF THE *HUNTSMAN V HEAVILIN* SUIT
FILED BY ATTORNEY RESTIVO

IN THE CIRCUIT COURT OF THE SIXTEENTH
JUDICIAL CIRCUIT
IN AND FOR MONROE COUNTY, FLORIDA
AARON R. HUNTSMAN AND
WILLIAM LEE JONES,
Plaintiffs,

v.

AMY HEAVILIN, as Clerk of the Courts of
Monroe County, Florida, in her official
capacity,
Defendant.
CASE NO.
COMPLAINT FOR DECLARATORY AND
INJUNCTIVE RELIEF
INTRODUCTION

1. This is an action brought by a same-sex couple residing in Key West, Monroe County, Florida who wish to join in marriage in their home state, but who applied for and were denied a marriage license by Amy Heavilin, Office of the Clerk of the Courts in Key West, Florida on April 1,2014, under the Florida laws that exclude same-sex couples from marriage. (See attached). The Plaintiffs allege that Florida's categorical exclusion of all same-sex couples from marriage deny same-sex couples, including Plaintiffs and their families, the fundamental rights, dignities and equalities guaranteed to all persons by the United States Constitution.

2. In this action, Plaintiffs challenge the constitutionality of the Florida laws that exclude same-sex couples from marriage. *See* Art . I, § 27, Fla. Const.; Fla. Stat. §§ 741.04,741.212. Florida's refusal to permit same-sex couples to marry violates a myriad of constitutionally guaranteed rights. This Court should so declare and issue a mandatory injunction requiring Defendant to issue marriage licenses to the Plaintiff Couple.

3. Plaintiffs are Aaron R. Huntsman and William Lee Jones. It is the desire and commitment of this same-sex couple to publicly and officially solemnize and solidify their relationship by entering into a legally binding marriage in the state of Florida; a contractual commitment, one to the other; and in so doing, sharing in the protections , obligations, rights, responsibilities and securities that the Florida laws of marriage afford.

4. The Plaintiffs are residents of Key West, Monroe County, Florida. They are respectful, productive and contributing members of their community. They come before the Court with various backgrounds, experiences, professions and educations. These individuals have made a life-long commitment to each other.

5. "The freedom to marry has long been recognized as one of the vital personal rights essential to the orderly pursuit of happiness by free men" that is protected by the Due Process Clause. *Loving* v. *Virginia* , 388 U.S. 1, 12 (1967).

6. "While states do have a legitimate interest in regulating and promoting marriage, the fundamental right to marry belongs to the individual. The restrictions imposed on marriage must nonetheless comply with the United States Constitution. " *Obergefell* v. *Wymyslo* , United States District

Court, Southern Division of Ohio, Case NO.1: 13-cv-501

footnote 10 at page 19 (December 23, 2013), citing *Hodgson v. Minnesota*, 497 U.S. 417,435 (1990). (See attached) .

7. Therefore , "the regulations of constitutionally protected decisions, such as where a person shall reside or whom he or she shall marry, must be predicated on legitimate state concerns other than disagreement with the choice the individual has made." *Hodgson at* 435 (1990).

8. These Plaintiffs are similarly situated to other same-sex couples across the state of Florida whose fundamental rights are infringed by the denial of the basic rights, privileges and protections of marriage for themselves and their families.

9. Under Art. I, § 27, Fla. Const., marriage is defined as "the legal union of only one man and one woman as husband and wife, [and] no other legal union that is treated as marriage or the substantial equivalent thereof shall be valid or recognized ."

10. Florida Statute § 741.04(1) provides that "[n]o county court judge or clerk of the circuit court in this state shall issue a license for the marriage of any person unless there shall be first presented and filed with him or her an affidavit in writing , signed by both parties to the marriage, providing the social security numbers or any other available identification numbers of each party, made and subscribed before some person authorized by law to administer an oath, reciting the true and correct ages of such parties; unless both such parties shall be over the age of 18 years, except as provided in §, 741.0405; and unless one party is a male and the other party is a female." Emphasis added.

11. Florida Statute § 741.212(1) provides that "[m]arriages

between persons of the same sex entered into in any jurisdiction, whether within or outside the State of Florida,

HUNTSMAN AND JONES v. HEAVILIN Page 3 of 19

the United States, or any other jurisdiction, either domestic or foreign, or any other place or location , or **relationships between persons of the same sex which are treated as marriages** in any jurisdiction, whether within or outside the State of Florida, the United States, or any other jurisdiction, either domestic or foreign, or any other place or location , **are not recognized for any purpose in this** state. " Emphasis added .

12. In addition to stigmatizing a portion of Florida 's population as less than full citizens, Florida's prohibition on marriage of same-sex couples deprives those couples of critically important rights and responsibilities which married couples rely upon to secure their marriage commitment and safeguard their families. By way of example, and without limitation , same-sex partners are denied:

A: The right to be supported after marriage. In *Killian v. Lawson* , 387 So. 2d 960, 962 (Fla. 1980) the Court held that even though divorced, the husband must, by court order, continue to support his ex-wife. This duty arose out of a family relationship. The purpose of alimony is to prevent a dependent party from becoming a public charge or an object of charity. This right is not available to same-sex partners whose long-term relationships end after many years together.

B: The right of a the legal parent of a child born to a spouse during marriage. In *Florida Dept. of Revenue v. Cummings*, 895 So. 2d 405 (Fla. 2005), the Court held that a legal father is an indispensable party in an action to determine paternity and to place support obligations on another man unless it is conclusively established that the legal father's rights to the child have been divested by some earlier judgment. When a child is born to a same-sex couple , only the biological or adoptive parent is recognized as the legal parent. However, Florida courts are moving in the right direction, finding that

HUNTSMAN AND JONES v. HEAVILIN Page 4 of 19

Florida's assisted reproduction statute § 742.13(2) was unconstitutional due to violations of the (1) due process clause of the U.S. Constitution; (2) the due process claques and privacy provision of the Florida constitution ; (3) the federal equal protection clause; and (4) Florida's equal protection clause. *D.M.T v. TM.H.,* 2013 WL 5942278. In this case, the Court found that the statute violated state and federal equal protection clauses by denying same-sex couples the statutory protection against automatic relinquishment of parental rights that it afforded to heterosexual unmarried couples seeking to utilize identical reproductive technologies. *Id.* at *2.

C. The right to make medical decisions for an ill or incapacitated spouse without an advance health care directive. Under Florida Statute § 765.401, a same sex "spouse" would be the second to last person appointed as the proxy; only a clinical social worker licensed pursuant to chapter 491 ranks below a same-sex "spouse" as defined by statute as "a close friend. " This obstacle has created grave and frustrating scenes for same-sex couples facing end-of-life decisions.

D: The right to spousal insurance coverage and benefits, when spousal benefits are otherwise available. State of Florida employees are offered health insurance benefits for their dependents, including spouses who "are of the opposite sex to whom you are legally married." (See attached). Same-sex partners of Florida state employees are purposely excluded from enjoying the benefits afforded to heterosexual partners of other state employees.

E: In accordance with the requirements to obtain Social Security benefits, Medicare/Medicaid and Family Medical Leave Act, one has to be legally married to the individual to partake of these benefits. Although the United State Supreme Court has

HUNTSMAN AND JONES v. HEAVILIN Page 5 of 19

ruled that federal benefits may not be withheld from same-sex couples, since a legal marriage is a requirement, same-sex partners who have cohabited for years would be and are discriminated against if they live in a state that does not recognize same-sex marriages. See *U.S.* v. *Windsor,* 133 S.Ct. 2675 (2013).

F: The right to a court-ordered equitable distribution of property. Under Fla. Stat. § 61.075, in order for an individual to assert the right to a court-ordered equitable distribution of property upon dissolution of marriage, an individual would have to been legally married . Since same-sex marriage is not legal in Florida , nor is it recognized by Florida, same-sex "spouses " are not given this right.

G: The right to receive certain workers' compensation benefits for a deceased spouse who has died as a result of a work-related accident. Fla. Stat. § 440 .16 gives the surviving spouse of a deceased spouse the right to receive certain worker's compensation benefits as a result of a work-related accident. In order to qualify for this right, the individual has to be in a legal marriage that is recognized by Florida. Even the children, siblings and grandchildren of the deceased are afforded this right but not same-sex "spouses".

H: The right to inherit a share of the estate of a spouse who dies without a will. Under Fla. Stat.§ 732.102, if a deceased spouse dies without a will , the surviving spouse's right to inherit a share of the estate is protected. This protection at minimum is one half of the estate and is only available if the deceased and the spouse were in a legal marriage that is recognized by Florida. A same-sex "spouse's right is not protected under this statute. The lack of legal recognition for a same-sex spouse has resulted in estate planning challenges and probate contests.

HUNTSMAN AND JONES v. HEAVILIN Page 6 of 19

I: The right to receive an elective share of the estate of a spouse who died with a will. Under Fla. Stat.§ 733 .301, the surviving spouse has the right to receive an elective share of the estate of a spouse who died with a will. This right is only afforded to a spouse who is in a legal marriage that is recognized by the State of Florida. Since Florida does not recognize same-sex marriages, the same-sex "spouse" is not offered this right.

J: The right to priority in appointment as the personal representative of the estate of a spouse who dies without a will. A same-sex surviving "spouse" does not have the right to priority in appointment as the personal representative of the estate of a spouse who dies without a will. Under Fla. Stat. § 733 .301, only the spouse of a legally recognized marriage is offered this right.

K: The privilege not to have a spouse testify in a court proceeding about confidential communications made during the marriage. In a legally recognized marriage in the State of Florida, a spouse has the right not to have the other spouse testify in a court proceeding about confidential communications during the marriage according to Fla. Stat. 90.504(1): "Husband-wife privilege-A spouse has a privilege during and after the marital relationship to refuse to disclose, and to prevent another from disclosing, communications which were intended to be made in confidence between the spouses while they were husband and wife. " A same-sex couple is not afforded this very important privilege and protection .

L: The right of spouses of military personnel to be eligible to participate in the state 's employment advocacy and assistance program for military spouses. In the State of Florida, under Fla. Stat. 445.055, a spouse of military personnel, in a legally

HUNTSMAN AND JONES v. HEAVILIN Page 7 of 19

recognized marriage, has the right to be eligible to participate in the state's employment advocacy and assistance program for military spouses. Since the State of Florida does not recognize same-sex marriages, the same-sex spouse of a military person would be prevented from seeking assistance from the state's employment advocacy and assistance program for military spouses .

10. By denying a marriage licenses to same-sex couples, Florida infringes upon these individuals' fundamental rights and basic life choices, denying them the public recognition and numerous legal benefits of marriage.

11. "Because a person's sexual orientation is so integral an aspect of one's identity, it is not appropriate to require a person to repudiate or change his or her sexual orientation in order to avoid discriminatory treatment." *In re Marriage Cases*, 183 P.3d. 384,442 (Cal. 2008).

12. "...for centuries there have been powerful voices to

condemn homosexual conduct as immoral. The condemnation has been shaped by religious beliefs , conceptions of right and acceptable behavior, and respect for the traditional family. For many persons these are not trivial concerns but profound and deep convictions accepted as ethical and moral principles to which they aspire and which thus determine the course of their lives. These considerations do not answer the question before us, however. **The issue is whether the majority may use the power of the State to enforce these views on the whole society through operation of the criminal law. "Our obligation is to define the liberty of all, not to mandate our own moral code."** *Lawrence v. Texas, 539* U.S. 558, 571 (2003), *citing Planned Parenthood of Southeastern Pa. v. Casey,* 505 U. S. 833, 850 (1992). Emphasis added.

13. The actions of the Defendant Clerk of the Courts, as well as the Florida Constitution and laws, cannot survive any level of constitutional scrutiny because they

HUNTSMAN AND JONES v. HEAVILIN Page 8 of 19

do not have a rational relationship to any legitimate government interest. Specifically, these prohibitions do not survive the heightened scrutiny required because they infringe upon a fundamental constitutional right and serve to discriminate on the basis of sex and sexual orientation.

14. The fact that the same-sex marriage ban was approved by a majority of the Florida electorate does not make it "constitutional." "The lower courts are applying the Supreme Court's decision [in *Windsor*], as they must, and the question is presented whether a state can do what the federal government cannot - Le., discriminate against same-sex couples .. ... simply because the majority of voters don't like homosexuality (or at least didn't in 2004). Under the

Constitution of the United States, the answer is no. "
Obergefell at page 3. Emphasis added.

15. "The very purpose of a Bill of Rights was to withdraw certain subjects from the vicissitudes of political controversy, to place them beyond the reach of majorities and officials and to establish them as legal principles to be applied by the courts. One's right to life, liberty, and property, to free speech, a free press, freedom of worship and assembly, and other fundamental rights may not be submitted to vote; they depend on the outcome of no elections." *W Virginia State Bd. of Educe.* v. *Barnette,* 319 U.S. 624,638 (1943). (Emphasis added).

16. "[R]egardless of whoever finds favor in the eyes of the most recent majority, the guarantee of equal protection must prevail." *DeBoer* v. *Snyder,* U.S. District Court , Eastern District of Michigan, Southern Division, Case No. 12-CV-10285, March 21, 2014 at page 30. (See attached).

HUNTSMAN AND JONES v. HEAVILIN Page 9 of 19

17. "[N]o hypothetical justification can overcome the clear primary purpose and practical effect of the marriage bans....to disparage and demean the dignity of same-sex couples in the eyes of the State and the wider community. When the primary purpose and effect of a law is to harm an identifiable group, the fact that the law may also incidentally serve some other neutral governmental interest cannot save it from unconstitutionality." *Windsor,* 133 S.Ct. at 2696.

18. "The Constitution 's guarantee of equality 'must at the very least mean that a bare congressional desire to harm a politically unpopular group cannot' justify disparate treatment of that group." *Windsor,* 133 S.Ct. at 2693, citing *Dept. of Agriculture* v. *Moreno,* 413 U.S. 528, 534-535 (1973).

18. Plaintiffs bring this suit pursuant to 42 U.S.C. § 1983 and Fla. Stat. § 26.012(2)(c) for declaration and injunctive relief against Defendant Clerk of the Court. Specifically, Plaintiffs seek: (a) a declaration that Florida's laws and the Defendant's actions preventing same-sex couples from marrying violate the Due Process Clause and the Equal Protection Clause of the Fourteenth Amendment to the United States Constitution ; and (b) a permanent mandatory injunction preventing Defendant Clerk of the Courts from denying same-sex couples the right to marry and requiring Defendant Clerk of the Courts to uses marriage licenses to the plaintiff couples and other similarly situated same-sex couples.

19. "The history of discrimination against gay and lesbian individuals has been both severe and pervasive. In 1952, Congress prohibited gay men and women from entering the country. In 1953, President Eisenhower issued an executive order requiring the discharge of gay people from all federal employment and mandating that all defense contractors and other private corporations with federal contracts ferret out and fire all homosexual employees, a policy which remained

HUNTSMAN AND JONES v. HEAVILIN Page 10 of 19

in place until 1975. Even then, federal agencies were free to discriminate based on sexual orientation until President Clinton issued the first executive order forbidding such hiring discrimination in 1998. After World War II, known homosexual service members were denied GI Bill benefits , and later, when other people with undesirable discharges had their benefits restored, the Veterans Administration refused to restore them to gay people." "Until the Supreme Court's *Lawrence* decision in 2003, consensual homosexual conduct was criminalized in many states. In the mid-twentieth century, bars in major American cities posted signs telling potential gay customers they were not welcome, and raids on gay bars in this period were 'a fact of life, a danger every patron risked by walking through the door. Until 2011 , homosexuals could not openly serve in the military, and the military still criminalizes sodomy today.'" "These are just some of the most egregious examples of discrimination against gays and lesbians at the hands of both federal and state governments, their officials, and one of the two primary political parties in our country, and based on these examples alone, 'it is easy to conclude that homosexuals have suffered a history of discrimination ." *Obergefell* at page 29-30, footnotes omitted. See also *DeLeon, Dimetman et al v. Perry, et ai*, U.S.D.C., Western Division of Texas, SA-13-CA 982OLG (February 26,2014). (See attached).

JURISDICTION

20. This Court has subject matter jurisdiction over this equitable action pursuant to Fla. Stat. § 26.012(2)(c) .

21. Venue is proper in the 16th Judicial Circuit and Monroe County pursuant to Fla. Stat. § 47.011 because this cause of action accrued in this county and the Defendant Clerk of the Courts resides in this county.

PLAINTIFFS

HUNTSMAN AND JONES v. HEAVILIN Page 11 of 19

22. Plaintiffs, Aaron Huntsman and William Lee Jones, have been in a committed same-sex relationship since June 10, 2003. Both men work in the tourist service industry in Key West, where they also reside together. Working together and living together, the couple proudly say that they spend about 95% of their time together all day every

day and night.

23. On June 11, 2004, the couple went to Las Vegas, Nevada in an attempt to get legally married. However, they were turned down because there was no recognition for same-sex marriages in Nevada. However, they did take advantage of having a civil commitment ceremony. Their ceremony was broadcast live over the Internet as one of the first gay "marriages". Plaintiffs do not wish to travel to another state in order to obtain a legal marriage. They already feel in their hearts that they are a married couple in their eyes and in the eyes of God. They desire to have their marriage legalized and recognized in the state of Florida where they reside.

DEFENDANT

24. The Defendant Amy Heavilin is the Clerk of the Courts for Monroe County, Florida. Defendant Heavilin, in her official capacity, is responsible for issuing and recording marriage licenses through the application process. Defendant Heavilin is a person within the meaning of 42 U.S.C. § 1983 and was acting under color of Florida law at all times relevant to this complaint. Defendant Heavilin's official residence is Monroe County. She is sued in her official capacity.

25. Defendant Heavilin and her staff, in their official capacity, are sworn to determine the qualification of applicants for Florida marriage licenses and to issue marriage

TRANSCRIPT OF THE
HUNTSMAN V. HEAVILIN HEARING

1

IN THE CIRCUIT COURT OF THE SIXTEENTH
JUDICIAL CIRCUIT
IN AND FOR MONROE COUNTY, FLORIDA
CASE NO.: 2014-CA-0305-K
AARON R. HUNTSMAN AND
WILLIAM LEE JONES,
Plaintiffs,

v.

AMY HEAVILIN, as Clerk of the Courts
of Monroe County, Florida, in her
official capacity,
Defendants.

_____/

TRANSCRIPT OF PROCEEDINGS
PLAINTIFF'S MOTION FOR SUMMARY JUDGMENT
DATE TAKEN: July 7, 2014
TIME: 9:40 - 11:10 A.M.
PLACE: Plantation Key Courthouse
88820 Overseas Highway
Tavernier, Florida 33070
BEFORE: Hon. Luis M. Garcia
Suzanne Ex, CVR-M, FPR
Certified Verbatim Reporter
Florida Professional Reporter

. .

1-888-311-4240
WWW.USLEGALSUPPORT.COM
2
APPEARANCES .
On Behalf of the Plaintiffs:
RESTIVO REILLY & VIGIL-FARINAS, LLC
103400 Overseas Highway, Suite 237
Key Largo, Florida 33037
(305) 453-4961 / Fax (305) 496-4131
bernadette@rrvflaw.com
elena@rrvflaw.com
tom@rrvflaw.com
BY: BERNADETTE RESTIVO, ESQUIRE
ELENA VIGIL-FARINAS, ESQUIRE
THOMAS L. HAMPTON, ESQUIRE
On Behalf of the Defendant:
MONROE COUNTY CLERK OF COURT &
COMPTROLLER
500 Whitehead Street, Suite 101
Key West, Florida 33040
(305) 292-3506 / Fax (305) 295-3970
rsaunders@monroe-clerk.com
BY: RON SAUNDERS, ESQUIRE
On Behalf of the State of Florida:
OFFICE OF THE ATTORNEY GENERAL, STATE
OF FLORIDA
PL-01, The Capitol
Tallahassee, Florida 32399-1050
(850) 414-3681 / Fax (850) 410-2672
Adam.Tanenbaum@myfloridalegal.com
BY: ADAM S. TANENBAUM, ESQUIRE
On Behalf of the Amicus Curiae:
LIBERTY COUNSEL
Post Office Box 540774

Orlando, Florida 32854

(800) 671-1776 / Fax (407) 875-0770

mat@LC.org

BY: MATHEW D. STAVER, ESQUIRE

Also Present:

AARON R. HUNTSMAN

WILLIAM LEE JONES

. --ooOoo-- .

1-888-311-4240

WWW.USLEGALSUPPORT.COM

3

INDEX OF PROCEEDINGS Page

PLAINTIFF'S MOTION FOR SUMMARY JUDGMENT

. .

1-888-311-4240

WWW.USLEGALSUPPORT.COM

4

1 (The proceeding commenced with all parties present

2 as follows:)

3 THE BAILIFF: Judge Luis Garcia presiding.

4 THE COURT: Good morning, please be seated.

5 Ladies and gentlemen, I'll remind you that this is

6 a court of law and you should act accordingly. Any

7 outbursts or disruptions shall result in your immediate

8 removal by the court deputies.

9 The Court now calls the case of Huntsman and Jones

10 vs. the Clerk of Monroe County and the State of

Florida.

11 Will all the parties please announce their presence for
12 the record.
13 MS. RESTIVO: Bernadette Restivo and Elena Vigil-
14 Farinas and Thomas Hampton on behalf of Restivo, Reilly
15 and Vigil-Farinas. We're present here in court today
16 with our clients Aaron Huntsman and William Lee Jones.
17 THE COURT: Good morning.
18 MS. VIGIL-FARINAS: Good morning, Judge.
19 THE COURT: Defendants, please.
20 MR. SAUNDERS: Ron Saunders on behalf of the Monroe
21 County Clerk of Court.
22 MR. TANENBAUM: Adam Tanenbaum, Office of the
23 Attorney General on behalf of the State of Florida.
24 MR. STAVER: Mat Staver with Liberty Counsel
25 representing the Amicus, the Florida Family Action, the
1-888-311-4240
WWW.USLEGALSUPPORT.COM
5
1 Florida Democratic League and People United to Lead the
2 Struggle for Equality.
3 THE COURT: Thank you. Good morning.
4 All parties have requested time before the Court.
5 Counsel for the Plaintiff, you've requested an hour.
6 How would you like to divide your time?
7 MS. RESTIVO: Your Honor, I will do the opening for
8 approximately 45 minutes, and then Elena Vigil-Farinas
9 will do the closing for the remaining time.
10 THE COURT: And, for the Defendants. Mr. Saunders,
11 how much time would you like?
12 MR. SAUNDERS: Approximately two minutes.

13 THE COURT: Counsel for the State?

14 MR. TANENBAUM: Your Honor, five or ten minutes

15 should be sufficient for us.

16 THE COURT: Yes, sir.

17 MR. STAVER: Your Honor, we're here as Amicus, so

18 we're at the Court's discretion, but if we had 45

19 minutes, that would be fine for us.

20 THE COURT: I have reviewed all the pleadings and

21 the case law. I will not be issuing an order from the

22 bench today. I will take it under advisement and issue

23 a ruling shortly, within a short period of time.

24 Counsel for the Plaintiff, whenever you're ready.

25 MS. RESTIVO: Thank you, Your Honor. I'm having a

1-888-311-4240

WWW.USLEGALSUPPORT.COM

6

1 little trouble with this microphone. Thank you.

2 Good morning, Judge.

3 THE COURT: Good morning.

4 MS. RESTIVO: Just for the record, I am Bernadette

5 Restivo.

6 On April 1st, 2014, Aaron Huntsman and Lee Jones

7 went to the Monroe County Clerk of Court's office in Key

8 West to obtain a marriage license. Aaron and Lee have

9 been in a committed, loving relationship for 11 years.

10 It was their hope to get married on their anniversary of

11 June 10th of 2014. However, they were turned away by

12 the County Clerk, having been denied a marriage license.

13 The reason being, as we all know, is that Aaron and Lee

14 are both males and Florida laws, including the Florida

15 Constitution and the Florida Statutes 741.04 and

16 741.212, prohibit their marriage.

17 We believe that the Florida Keys in Monroe County

18 is a proper site for this same-sex marriage to be heard.

19 We who reside in the Florida Keys understand the

20 tradition and the comfort of living in a community which

21 accepts all people from all over the globe living in a

22 variety of lifestyles.

23 Even before Ernest Hemingway and Tennessee Williams

24 descended upon the Keys to write their masterpieces, and

25 craftsmen and other writers and artists, along with

1-888-311-4240

WWW.USLEGALSUPPORT.COM

7

1 fishermen and divers, and even U.S. Presidents and a

2 myriad of other folks, have been attracted to the

3 accommodating, forgiving and accepting Florida Keys.

4 Clearly, it's the Florida Keys which should be the first

5 and foremost in reversing this invasive and hurtful

6 discrimination which demeans so many of our citizens.

7 This is why we're asking for your ruling finding

8 Florida's same-sex marriage ban to be unconstitutional.

9 Before I address the substantive content of the

10 motion, I would like to address any procedural issues

11 that might be raised by our opponents.

12 First, this case is properly before the Court on

13 summary judgment. The parties to this suit have agreed

14 that there are no disputed material facts and the Amicus

15 has to find this case as he takes it. The Amicus is not

16 a party, nor did they attempt to become a party.

17 There's no need for an evidentiary hearing to

18 consider relative alleged sides, because Florida courts

19 have already considered the relevant sides and concluded

20 that there is no rational basis for treating same-sex
21 and opposite-sex parents any differently, as we saw in
22 the adoption of XXG decided by the Third District Court
23 of Appeals, and also cited by the Florida Supreme Court
24 in DMT. That is now a matter of law, binding upon us.
25 There is no reason to have an evidentiary hearing on
1-888-311-4240
WWW.USLEGALSUPPORT.COM
8
1 that issue.
2 In XXG, the question was whether homosexual couples
3 should be denied the right to adopt a child. After
4 lengthy hearings, the Court concluded that there was no
5 rational basis to prevent a homosexual from adopting a
6 child and set aside that statute.
7 Moreover, one of the experts cited in the Amicus,
8 Sociologist Mark Regnerus, was found to be, quote,
9 "entirely unbelievable and not worthy of serious
10 consideration," after a length evidentiary hearing in
11 the Federal District Court of Michigan, and he has been
12 disregarded by his own university.
13 The Amicus may suggest that laws that are based on
14 animus are for a factual issue. But, we believe, no,
15 it's a legal issue to be determined based on the text
16 and the legislative history of the laws, just as the
17 Supreme Court held in Windsor. The court there found
18 that animus based on the text, purpose and legislative
19 history of DOMA did not require any evidentiary hearing.
20 Whether a law was passed for an improper purpose is a
21 legal question, just like any other question of
22 statutory interpretation.
23 I begin my legal argument with this succinct

24 statement from the Southern District of Ohio's Federal
25 Court in Henry vs. Himes, decided in April 2014. "All

9

1 practicing attorneys, as well as the vast majority of
2 citizens in this country, are fully aware that
3 unconstitutional laws cannot stand, even when passed by
4 popular vote."
5 In light of the June 2013 Windsor case, we are now
6 faced with the decision of whether the State of Florida
7 can do what the federal government cannot do;
8 discriminate against same-sex couples.
9 And, I'm going to depart from my script for just a
10 moment, because I think I would like to address the
11 white elephant in the room. That being, the argument of
12 the State regarding the case of Baker.
13 THE COURT: Uh-huh.
14 MS. RESTIVO: Baker was a 1971 case that came up in
15 the State of Minnesota. It was an appeal of the same-
16 sex marriage ban in Minnesota. The case went to the
17 United States Supreme Court, but was summarily dismissed
18 on a jurisdictional issue. The State argues that since
19 the case hasn't yet been overruled, that it should be
20 binding as precedent. And, I'm going to get into why
21 all of the issues as far as doctrinal developments,
22 which have occurred since the argument was made in
23 Baker, would allow this Court, as well as the myriad of
24 other courts that have decided prior to us, to discard
25 Baker.

10

1 But, my learned partner, Elena, yesterday we were
2 meeting and we were going over this whole issue of Baker
3 and arguing just for the heck of arguing, trying to poke
4 holes as to why, why is this such a problematic case for
5 us? Why did Windsor not mention Baker? So, we kept --
6 we were arguing back and forth and my argument was,
7 Baker is a Minnesota case. Baker is a Minnesota
8 opinion. It applies in Minnesota. And then, it dawned
9 on us; does it? So, we went to Minnesota.
10 Minnesota reversed Baker, on their own, prior to
11 the Windsor ruling. In May of 2013, based on the
12 rejection of the popular vote in Minnesota in November
13 of 2012, the legislature in Minnesota rewrote their
14 marriage laws, which I have copies of the statutes here,
15 removing any ban for same-sex marriage. Baker not only
16 doesn't apply in the United States, it doesn't apply in
17 Minnesota. That's the reason the United States Supreme
18 Court, we suggest, didn't mention Baker; it's been
19 reversed.
20 There has also been such a myriad of doctrinal
21 developments in our country from the time that Baker was
22 brought forth in 1971. When you think of it, 1971 was
23 the year that equal protection was given to women.
24 Think how far we've come just from that perspective. I
25 know I was 11 years old. And, the changes that we've

1-888-311-4240
WWW.USLEGALSUPPORT.COM
11

1 seen -- not, we're not just talking about the last
2 couple of years of developments within sexual
3 orientation or protection of sex. That's this whole
4 society where we have brought forth equality across the

5 board. I don't think we need to sit and list all the

6 doctrinal developments that have occurred since then.

7 In 1980, the voters of Florida passed what is now

8 Article I, Section 23 of the Florida Constitution, the

9 Right to Privacy Amendment. There's only ten states in

10 our country that have placed the Right to Privacy

11 Amendment in their state constitutions. And, we will

12 show, through our argument and what we presented to the

13 Court in our response, is that that right to privacy

14 protection within our Florida Constitution should

15 obliviate [sic] Section 27 on the same-sex marriage ban

16 as being totally unconstitutional.

17 The slogan that we see being used, "Respect Our

18 Vote," should also include the vote that was taken in

19 1980. The right to privacy for all Floridians should

20 and must trump the intrusive and demeaning marriage ban

21 aimed at oppressing the fundamental right to privacy for

22 a select few Floridians. The constitution's guarantee

23 of equality must, at the very least, mean that a fair

24 congressional desire to harm a politically unpopular

25 group cannot justify disparate treatment of that group,

1-888-311-4240

WWW.USLEGALSUPPORT.COM

12

1 as held by the Windsor court.

2 The United States Supreme Court said, "The very

3 purpose of a Bill of Rights was to withdraw from certain

4 subjects from the vicissitude of political controversy,

5 to place them beyond the reach of the majority of

6 officials and to establish legal principles to be

7 applied by the courts."

8 And, most importantly, the U.S. Supreme Court said,

9 "The United States Constitution guarantees that all
10 citizens have certain fundamental rights. These rights
11 vest in every person over whom the constitution has
12 authority and, because they are so important, an
13 individual's fundamental right may not be submitted to
14 vote. They depend on the outcome of no election."
15 While the State argues that the regulation of
16 domestic relations is an area for the State, and it's
17 long been a province of the State, the Supreme Court has
18 ruled that state laws defining and regulating marriage
19 must respect the constitutional right of persons. State
20 regulations of marriage are subject to constitutional
21 guarantees.
22 Section 27, with the same-sex marriage ban in the
23 Florida Statutes, denies same-sex couples the right to
24 enter into a marriage contract, which not only violate
25 the Equal Protection Clause of the Fourteenth Amendment
1-888-311-4240
WWW.USLEGALSUPPORT.COM
13
1 of the United States, but they also violate the Florida
2 Constitution and the laws as interpreted by the Florida
3 Supreme Court.
4 Our argument today focuses on the
5 unconstitutionality of the same-sex marriage amendment
6 and the statutes under Florida law. The State's primary
7 argument is that Florida courts should not review the
8 constitutionality of the 27th Amendment because it was a
9 majority vote of the people. But, the State misses the
10 point in so many ways.
11 First, the State argues that the courts should not
12 review the constitutionality of the amendment, because

13 it was passed by majority vote. Ever since Marbury vs.
14 Madison, it's been a proper and traditional exercise of
15 judicial review for courts to analyze and decide the
16 constitutionality of laws. It's certainly this judicial
17 branch of Florida's obligation to review the amendment
18 with context of the Florida Constitution. To elevate
19 and sanctify the outcome of an election without thought
20 to the constitutionality of its ramifications is an
21 extraordinarily contrary premise to American
22 jurisprudence.
23 Second, the State conveniently overlooks the fact
24 that the voters in 1980, passed the Right to Privacy
25 Amendment and, unlike the same-sex marriage ban, the

1-888-311-4240
WWW.USLEGALSUPPORT.COM
14

1 Right to Privacy Amendment has survived numerous
2 judicial reviews at every level. The right to privacy
3 has been defined, interpreted and applied by the Florida
4 Supreme Court.
5 Third, while the State's argument that the right to
6 same-sex marriage is not a fundamental right, we believe
7 that previous rulings from the Florida Supreme Court
8 rule otherwise, and that's why we are asking this Court
9 to apply a heightened-scrutiny test under Florida law.
10 Fourth, even when the State's argument that this is
11 a rational-based test case, the State has asserted no
12 rational basis, nor have they articulated any legitimate
13 government interest.
14 Previous courts across the country have already
15 held that suggested rationalizations for disparate
16 treatment for same-sex couples such as procreation,
17 protection of children and tradition and continuity of
18 laws have all been found to fall short of providing a

19 rational basis.

20 The Third District Court of Appeals in XXG

21 considered the issue as to whether there was a rational

22 relationship to exclude homosexuals from adopting

23 children. The ruling in XXG is clearly, no.

24 The Amicus may suggest some rational basis for this

25 amendment; procreation being one of them. Procreation

1-888-311-4240

WWW.USLEGALSUPPORT.COM

15

1 is not a prerequisite in Florida for a marriage license.

2 Opposite-sex couples can choose not to have children, or

3 they may be infertile, or they may be past the age of

4 childbearing; but, yet, we don't deny them a marriage

5 license.

6 In DMT, the Florida Supreme Court stated that,

7 "Although the right to procreate has long been described

8 as one of the basic civil rights individuals hold,

9 advances in science and technology now provide

10 innumerable ways for traditional and nontraditional

11 couples alike to conceive a child, and we conclude, in

12 doing so, to exercise their inalienable rights to enjoy

13 and defend life and liberty and to pursue happiness."

14 Thus, the right to procreation for nontraditional

15 couples is a basic civil right in Florida. It would

16 make no sense at all to allow homosexuals to adopt

17 children and to procreate using assisted reproduction,

18 but not allow them to marry.

19 The courts have ruled on the similar arguments that

20 are coming from the Amicus and have recently held that

21 these arguments are not those of serious people.

22 Tradition alone cannot form the rational basis for a

23 law, as the Supreme Court has held on numerous

24 occasions. They stated that the fact that a particular

25 discrimination has been traditional is even more of a

1 reason to be skeptical of its rationality.

2 The Court must be especially diligent in evaluating

3 the rationality of any classification involving a group

4 that's been subjected to a tradition of disfavor, for a

5 traditional classification is more likely to be used

6 without pausing to consider its justifications than is a

7 newly-created classification.

8 In overturning Bowers, the court, in Lawrence,

9 stated that, "Bowers made the broader point that, for

10 centuries, there have been powerful voices to condemn

11 homosexual conduct as immoral. The condemnation has

12 been shaped by religious beliefs, conceptions of right

13 and acceptable behavior, and respect for the traditional

14 family. For many persons, these are not trivial

15 concerns, but profound, deep convictions accepted as

16 ethical and moral principles to which they aspire and

17 which thus determine the course of their lives, but

18 these considerations do not answer the question before

19 us. The issue is whether the majority may use the power

20 of the state to enforce these views on the whole

21 society." Clearly, the answer in Lawrence is no.

22 Effects on children. Any suggestion of negative

23 ramifications for children of homosexual parents has

24 already been debunked by the Third District Court of

25 Appeals in XXG. Even the testimony of the so-called

1 experts was disregarded by the Court in finding that

2 there's no rational basis to prohibit homosexuals from

3 adopting children in Florida. The Court found it was a
4 violation of the Equal Protection Clause of the Florida
5 Constitution.
6 In D.M.T., the Florida Supreme Court ruled that the
7 State would be hard pressed to find a reason why a child
8 would not be better off having two loving parents in
9 their life, regardless of whether those parents are of
10 the same sex, than she would be by having one parent.
11 This court struck down this law discriminating against
12 same-sex couples in assisted reproduction. Again, it's
13 not logical for Florida to permit same-sex parents to
14 adopt a child, to create a child, but not allow them to
15 marry. To me, it suggests a violation of public policy.
16 We wanted to take a minute to consider the Florida
17 Constitution, the preamble to the Florida Constitution,
18 as follows: "We, the people of the State of Florida,
19 being grateful to Almighty God for our constitutional
20 liberty, in order to secure its benefits, perfect our
21 government, insure domestic tranquility, maintain public
22 order and guarantee equal civil and political rights to
23 all, do ordain and establish this constitution."
24 I thought it would be interesting to dissect that
25 preamble and see how it applies to the case here.
1-888-311-4240
WWW.USLEGALSUPPORT.COM
18
1 In order to secure its benefits. What benefits?
2 For my clients, there are no benefits. For this
3 minority group of same-sex couples, there's no
4 constitutionality or statutory benefits, only
5 detriments, and we listed them all in our motion for
6 summary judgment. The depravation of rights under the
7 State of Florida is closely analogous to Windsor and the
8 deprivation of federal benefits that were being

9 prevented to that couple from New York.

10 Article I, Section 1, State of Florida, says that,

11 quote, "All political power is inherent in the people.

12 The enunciation herein of certain rights shall not be

13 construed to deny or impair others retained by the

14 people." Article I, Section 1, was left intact by

15 Section 27, which singled out same-sex couples for the

16 purpose of disparate treatment. This is an

17 unconstitutional attempt to narrow the definition

18 equality. The exclusion of a minority for no rational

19 reason is very dangerous precedent.

20 As the court recently stated in Love vs. Beshear,

21 "Those opposed to same-sex marriage, by and large,

22 simply believe that the State has the right to adopt a

23 particular religious or traditional view of marriage,

24 regardless of how it may affect gay and lesbian persons.

25 But, as this court has respectfully explained, in

1-888-311-4240

WWW.USLEGALSUPPORT.COM

19

1 America, even sincere and long-held religious views do

2 not trump the constitutional rights of those who happen

3 to be outvoted."

4 Article I, Section 2 of the Florida Constitution

5 states that, quote, "All natural persons, female and

6 male alike, are equal before the law and have

7 inalienable rights, among which are the right to enjoy,

8 defend life and liberty and to pursue happiness."

9 The fact that Article 27 was -- I'm sorry, Section

10 27 was popular with the voters, does not protect it from

11 constitutional scrutiny as to federal and state rights.

12 The Due Process Clause of the Fourteenth Amendment

13 establishes that no state may deprive any person of

14 life, liberty or property without due process of law.

15 And, the freedom to marry has long been recognized as
16 one of the vital personal rights essential to the
17 orderly pursuit of happiness that is protected by the
18 Due Process Clause.
19 In light of the Windsor case, which held that the
20 federal government cannot refuse to recognize a valid
21 same-sex marriage, the question presented today to us
22 again is whether Florida can do what the federal
23 government cannot; discriminate against same-sex couples
24 simply because the a majority of voters don't like
25 homosexuality or at least didn't like it in 2008.
1-888-311-4240
WWW.USLEGALSUPPORT.COM
20
1 The right to enjoy and defend life and liberty.
2 All fundamental rights comprised within the term liberty
3 are protected by the federal constitution from invasion
4 by the states. And, neither the Bill of Rights or the
5 specific practices of states at the time of the adoption
6 of the Fourteenth Amendment mark the outer limits of the
7 substantive sphere of the Fourteenth Amendment. There
8 could be little doubt that the right to marry is a
9 fundamental liberty.
10 The marital relationship is older than the Bill of
11 Rights, older than our political parties, older than our
12 schools. Marriage is a coming together for better or
13 worse, hopefully enduring, and intimate to the degree of
14 being sacred. It's an association that promotes a way
15 of life, not causes; a harmony in living, not political
16 based; a bilateral loyalty, not commercial or social
17 projects. The United States Supreme Court has long
18 recognized that marriage is the most important relation

19 in life.

20 I could go on and on, on the Supreme Court cases

21 stating how marriage is a fundamental right, a most

22 important right in life.

23 The right to marry is a non-enumerated fundamental

24 right that is not written in the constitution. Its

25 constitutional significance arises from various

1-888-311-4240

WWW.USLEGALSUPPORT.COM

21

1 protected liberty interests such as the right to privacy

2 and freedom. Marital relationships are purely personal

3 in nature.

4 And, this brings us to Section 23, the Right to

5 Privacy Amendment in the constitution and how we believe

6 it trumps and disregards Section 27. It reads, "Every

7 natural person has the right to be let alone and free

8 from governmental intrusion into the person's private

9 life, except as otherwise provided herein."

10 Prior to the passage of the Right to Privacy

11 Amendment, the Florida Supreme Court ruled that various

12 intimate personal activities such as marriage,

13 procreation, contraception and family relationships fall

14 within the privacy interests recognized by the federal

15 constitution. That was in early 1980. The Right to

16 Privacy Amendment was passed in November of 1980.

17 Soon after the amendment's passage, the Florida

18 Supreme Court formally recognized that marriage and

19 family rights fall within the general right to privacy.

20 Since the people of this state exercised their

21 prerogative and enacted an amendment to the Florida

22 Constitution, it can only be concluded that the right to

23 privacy is much broader in scope than that of the
24 Federal Constitution. The Florida Supreme Court found
25 that Florida's privacy amendment provides an explicit

1 textual foundation for those privacy interests inherent
2 in the concept of liberty.
3 The Florida Supreme Court has interpreted Florida's
4 Constitution's privacy provision to provide greater
5 protection than is afforded by the Federal Constitution.
6 They have held that the right to privacy is an
7 independent, freestanding constitutional provision which
8 declares the fundamental right to privacy. Thus, once
9 it's determined that a citizen's privacy interest is
10 implicated, in this case, the fundamental right to marry
11 is a fundamental right under the privacy amendment, the
12 test shifts the burden to the State to prove that a
13 statute furthers a compelling state interest through the
14 least intrusive means.
15 To prevail over privacy rights, the State must show
16 that a statute furthers a compelling state interest
17 through the least intrusive means. And, in this case,
18 there has been no State interest articulated and no
19 argument for least intrusive means.
20 At this time, I'm going to reserve the remainder of
21 our time.
22 THE COURT: Thank you. Mr. Saunders.
23 MR. SAUNDERS: Thank you, Your Honor. Issuance of
24 marriage licenses is one of the many ministerial
25 functions of the Clerk's Office. Florida law clearly

1 states that the Clerk cannot issue a license unless one
2 of the parties is a male, the other party is a female.
3 Issuance of a license in violation of that would subject
4 the Clerk and Deputy Clerk to a misdemeanor of the first
5 degree, punishable by up to one year imprisonment or a
6 thousand-dollar fine.
7 The Plaintiff's are not challenging the Clerk's
8 interpretation of the law. They are challenging its
9 constitutionality. The State of Florida has intervened
10 to defend that constitutionality and the Clerk's Office
11 will abide by any decision of the Court on that issue.
12 THE COURT: Thank you. Counsel for the State of
13 Florida.
14 MR. TANENBAUM: May it please the Court. Your
15 Honor, approximately ten days ago the State filed a
16 memorandum of law urging the Court to deny the
17 Plaintiffs' summary judgment motion and to uphold the
18 validity of the statutory and constitutional provisions
19 being challenged here. The State relies on the
20 arguments made in that memorandum of law and I just
21 wanted to take a couple minutes to highlight some of the
22 key points.
23 THE COURT: All right.
24 MR. TANENBAUM: The United States Supreme Court in
25 Baker v. Nelson, and it's already been noted by Counsel,

1 unanimously determined that the definition of marriage
2 that is at issue here does not implicate the Due Process
3 Clause or the Equal Protection Clause of the Fourteenth
4 Amendment.

5 In the ensuing four decades since then, the United
6 States Supreme Court has not receded from that decision
7 and it has not expressly overruled that decision. Baker
8 v. Nelson remains binding precedent on this Court as it
9 does in every other lower court that is addressing the
10 federal constitutional arguments being made here.
11 It is not for this Court to guess as to what the
12 Supreme Court may do with respect to Baker. It is not
13 for this Court to determine whether the Supreme Court
14 has overruled that decision by implication. Rather, it
15 remains for this Court simply to respect the policy
16 decision made by the voters in 1997, through their
17 representatives in 2008, through the direct ballot.
18 Indeed, Your Honor, last year, the United States
19 Supreme Court reaffirmed each state's exclusive
20 authority to define marriage as a policy matter. And,
21 as I just noted, the voters exercised that right, the
22 Florida voters exercised that right and made a choice
23 through their elected representatives in 1997 and
24 through a super majority on the direct ballot in 2008.
25 THE COURT: Are you saying that trumps any
1-888-311-4240
WWW.USLEGALSUPPORT.COM
25

1 constitutionality scrutiny, that it doesn't still have
2 to pass the constitution, either Florida's or the U.S.?
3 MR. TANENBAUM: Well, Your Honor --
4 THE COURT: Because of the popular vote?
5 MR. TANENBAUM: Thank you, Your Honor. Your
Honor,
6 it is a federal question as to whether the Supreme --
7 and, the Supreme Court in Baker v. Nelson already
8 determined and has not overruled that decision in Baker
9 v. Nelson that the definition of marriage, and the

10 Minnesota definition is the same as the Florida

11 definition, does not implicate the Due Process Clause or

12 the Equal Protection Clause of the Fourteenth Amendment.

13 THE COURT: But, if the Florida Constitution

14 provides more protection than the United States

15 Constitution, then wouldn't we look at the Florida

16 Constitution to see if it violates the Florida

17 Constitution? Or, is it your opinion that the popular

18 vote trumps that and we don't have to go through that

19 exercise of looking at the Florida Constitution?

20 MR. TANENBAUM: Your Honor, the argument that the

21 plaintiffs have put forward with respect to the Florida

22 Constitution is that Section 23 somehow trumps Section

23 27. They would be hard pressed to point to the Court,

24 and in fact they have not pointed to the Court, any

25 decision where, any Florida decision where a subsequent

26

1 constitutional amendment, a subsequent amendment to the

2 Florida Constitution would be trumped by a prior

3 amendment to the Florida Constitution.

4 So, because Section 27 was passed after Section 23,

5 Section 27, the marriage definition at issue here, is

6 the will of the voters and that should be respected and

7 must be respected by this Court under existing U.S.

8 Supreme Court precedent until the Supreme Court says

9 otherwise.

10 THE COURT: So, there's never a constitutional

11 analysis to Section 27, in your opinion?

12 MR. TANENBAUM: Under the Federal Constitution,

13 Your Honor, the United States Supreme Court, the last
14 statement on that issue, was in Baker v. Nelson. That
15 is the United States Supreme Court and remains binding
16 precedent and this Court must follow it.
17 And, Your Honor, as I noted, it is not for this
18 Court to assess whether the policy decision made by the
19 voters, as late as 2008, is good policy or bad policy.
20 Rather, it is for this Court to simply follow binding
21 precedent, as I already noted, the United States Supreme
22 Court, in which gave voters of this state and the voters
23 of the State of Minnesota and every other state, to make
24 a determination on a controversial policy decision or
25 policy issue.
1-888-311-4240
WWW.USLEGALSUPPORT.COM
27
1 The voters exercised that right in the State of
2 Florida. That right, that determination should be
3 respected, just as they have retained the right to
4 participate in this debate and make a decision if they
5 change their minds down the road.
6 THE COURT: Well, wouldn't that same argument apply
7 to interracial marriages in our history? That the
8 popular vote at the time in different states in this
9 country were completely against interracial marriages?
10 MR. TANENBAUM: And, the United States Supreme
11 Court, five years prior to Baker v. Nelson, overruled
12 that and struck down that approach.
13 THE COURT: So, there was constitutional scrutiny
14 on that.
15 MR. TANENBAUM: Correct, just as there was in Baker
16 v. Nelson. The United States Supreme Court
unanimously
17 determined that the definition of marriage at issue here

18 does not implicate --

19 THE COURT: They dismissed it. They never

20 addressed the issue --

21 MR. TANENBAUM: The summary dismissal --

22 THE COURT: -- in Baker.

23 MR. TANENBAUM: I'm sorry.

24 THE COURT: Go ahead.

25 MR. TANENBAUM: The summary dismissal in Baker

v.

1-888-311-4240

WWW.USLEGALSUPPORT.COM

28

1 Nelson is binding. It is precedent. It is not simply a

2 jurisdictional matter. It has implications. It's an

3 implication that was followed by federal appellate

4 courts and district courts, including Judge Moody of the

5 Middle District of Florida as late as 2005, with respect

6 to Florida's definition of marriage.

7 Baker v. Nelson has implications and was followed

8 by the federal court. What Baker v. Nelson stands for,

9 continues to stand for, is that each -- is that the

10 State's definition of marriage does not implicate the

11 Due Process Clause or the Equal Protection Clause of
the

12 Fourteenth Amendment.

13 THE COURT: Did the State of Florida take a

14 position on the adoption of children by homosexuals
and

15 what was the State's position on that case?

16 MR. TANENBAUM: I'm sorry?

17 THE COURT: The State's position, when the case

18 went up, as to the adoption of children by homosexuals.

19 What position did the State of Florida take at the time,

20 do you know?

21 MR. TANENBAUM: I believe, DCF did not oppose that.

22 THE COURT: The State of Florida, DCF, the State of
23 Florida did not oppose it?

24 MR. TANENBAUM: That's correct.

25 THE COURT: Okay.

1-888-311-4240

WWW.USLEGALSUPPORT.COM

29

1 MR. TANENBAUM: At least on -- with respect to the
2 Third DCA opinion, Your Honor.

3 THE COURT: Finding that it was unconstitutional?

4 MR. TANENBAUM: To be clear, Your Honor, that's not
5 what's at issue here. What's at issue here is the
6 definition of marriage approved by a super-majority of
7 the voters in 2008, and we ask that the Court respect
8 that policy decision and follow binding precedent. And,
9 we ask that the Court deny the Plaintiffs' summary
10 judgment ,otion and uphold the constitutionality of the
11 statute and the constitutional provision being
12 challenged.

13 THE COURT: Thank you.

14 MR. TANENBAUM: Thank you.

15 THE COURT: Good morning.

16 MR. STAVER: Good morning, Your Honor. I'm Mat
17 Staver and I represent Florida Family Action, Florida
18 Democratic League and People United to Lead the Struggle
19 for Equality. I'm appearing on their behalf as Amicus.
20 Thank you for the opportunity to present arguments.

21 THE COURT: Yes, sir.

22 MR. STAVER: I want to address Baker, the standard
23 of review, the Article I, Section 23. But, I want to

24 begin first, before I address those issues, with some of
25 the original procedural issues in terms of the fact that
1-888-311-4240
WWW.USLEGALSUPPORT.COM
30
1 we're here on summary judgment. And, being here on
2 summary judgment, it is the burden of the Plaintiff to
3 prove that there are no disputes in the material facts.
4 There's been no stipulation to the facts. In fact,
5 the answer that has been filed by the Clerk of the Court
6 has denied, because of no knowledge of the allegations
7 that are in the complaint. And, most of the allegations
8 that are in the complaint are quotations or arguments
9 from different policies or case law, but not regarding a
10 lot pertaining to the individuals at questioning. The
11 only allegations that are really in the complaint is
12 that there's two individuals who sought to get a
13 marriage license and they weren't able to get a marriage
14 license in Florida. There's allegations about stigma,
15 but there's no information about that and there's no
16 affidavits to suggest or prove stigma.
17 The Plaintiff, at the time of the filing of the
18 motion, has to present those kinds of summary judgment
19 affidavits and evidence that would convince this Court
20 that, conclusively, there's no disputed material facts.
21 And, it is a very high burden, indeed, for the
22 Plaintiffs to reach. And, until and unless the
23 Plaintiff reaches and meets that burden, the burden
24 never shifts to the State. So, the State never even has
25 to bring forth the rational basis for this particular
1-888-311-4240
WWW.USLEGALSUPPORT.COM
31

1 argument of the law.

2 It is the Plaintiffs' duty to present to this

3 Court, information that just simply, conclusively to

4 this Court, suggests that we don't need a trial and, in

5 fact, they can skip all of the issues about whether

6 there's the best interest of children, we can skip all

7 of the other issues regarding animus and the motivation

8 of the Florida Marriage Protection Amendment and the

9 other laws that preceded it in '97 and '77, and then

10 going back to the very founding of Florida. All of that

11 is what the Plaintiff is asking this Court to do, but

12 the Plaintiff has not even presented that kind of

13 information to allow this Court to do that.

14 All we know is that they're citizens, they reside

15 in the Keys, they applied for a license and they didn't

16 get the license. That's it. I don't even know if that

17 has been agreed to with regards to the Clerk. But,

18 every other point that the Clerk has made in response to

19 that, the Clerk has denied.

20 And, the Plaintiffs say that there has been an

21 agreement to the stipulation of the facts. There is no

22 agreement for the stipulation of facts, and that is a

23 very basic premise for summary judgment. And, without

24 the Plaintiffs even meeting the very basic minimal

25 obligation to prove their burden, to show complicitly

1-888-311-4240

WWW.USLEGALSUPPORT.COM

32

1 that there's no issues of material fact and to negate

2 every rational basis that's been presented, which they

3 haven't even attempted to make every rational basis.

4 They've not presented any affidavits, they've not

5 presented any studies, they've presented no testimony,

6 they've made no allegations within their own complaint

7 or their affidavits to negate every rational basis.

8 And, even if there's just one rational basis, whether

9 they agree with it or not, the State prevails. And,

10 that's where we're here on this case for summary

11 judgment.

12 And, let me then move from that, because I don't

13 think the case is even ripe for summary judgment, with

14 all due respect to the Plaintiffs' request to bypass the

15 trial without presenting any admissible evidence that

16 negates rational basis or negates conclusively that

17 there's no issues of material facts.

18 But, with regards to the standard of review, the

19 standard of review is clearly rational basis. And even

20 in the Plaintiffs' complaint, in their count, they

21 allege rational basis. They don't allege strict

22 scrutiny, they don't allege intermediate scrutiny.

23 Their complaint that's here before this Court

24 specifically alleges rational basis. If they've never

25 met their burden, then the State doesn't have to prove

1-888-311-4240

WWW.USLEGALSUPPORT.COM

33

1 any rational basis. But, certainly, there's a lot of

2 rational bases for this.

3 And, in fact, if you look at the Supreme Court

4 decision in D.M.T., that particular decision of the

5 United States -- or, the U.S. -- Florida Supreme Court

6 in 2013, with regards to the Artificial Insemination

7 Statute, specifically used rational basis and said that

8 sexual orientation has not been determined to constitute

9 a protected class and, therefore, sexual orientation

10 does not provide an independent basis for using the

11 heightened scrutiny to review state action.

12 The Court cited to X.X.G., the adoption case, for

13 the proposition that in that particular case, they used
14 rational basis. Rational basis is clearly the standard
15 and rational basis requires Plaintiffs to negate every
16 potential rational basis, either that was adopted at the
17 time of the passage of these multiple laws throughout
18 the history of Florida, not just Article I, Section 23
19 or 27, but even any rational basis that could be
20 presented now.
21 We've presented several documents or affidavits and
22 information to the Court with regards to, first of all,
23 the motivation of Article I, Section 27, Florida
24 Marriage Protection Amendment, by John Stemberger.
John
25 Stemberger, in that affidavit, is the Chairman of the
1-888-311-4240
WWW.USLEGALSUPPORT.COM
34
1 Florida Family Action, the Amicus before this Court, and
2 was Chairman of the Marriage Initiative back in 2008,
3 that was ultimately passed by the voters.
4 In John Stemberger's affidavit, and it's the only
5 information before the Court with regards to the
6 motivation for that law or this constitutional
7 amendment, is that it was for the purpose of
8 strengthening marriage and for providing the best
9 optimal environment in which to raise children so that
10 they could have a home with a mom and a dad. That's
the
11 only information before this Court. So, the Plaintiffs
12 have not presented any information regarding animus or
13 any other motivation. That's the only evidence before
14 this Court.
15 We also have presented, Your Honor, other
16 information in regards to rational basis that I'll get

17 to in a few moments. But, with respect to, if I might
18 pause here just for a minute, with regards to the
19 Windsor case. In Windsor, Windsor did not change the
20 standard of review and it did not affect Baker vs.
21 Nelson. Windsor dealt with an interesting situation in
22 which the State of New York changed its definition to
23 include same-sex couples. But, before the Federal
24 Defense of Marriage Act was passed in 2006 [sic],
25 ultimately, one part of it said, for federal purposes,
1-888-311-4240
WWW.USLEGALSUPPORT.COM
35
1 the definition is the union of a man and a woman.
2 But, Windsor specifically says on page 2689 and
3 2690, "By history and tradition, the definition and
4 regulation of marriage, as will be discussed in more
5 detail, has been treated as being within the authority
6 and realm of the separate states."
7 And then, on 2691, Windsor states, "The definition
8 of marriage is the foundation of the state's broader
9 authority to regulate the subject of domestic relations
10 with respect to the protection of offspring, property
11 interests and the enforcement of marital
12 responsibilities."
13 On that same page, continuing, Windsor says, "The
14 significance of state responsibilities for the
15 definition and regulation of marriage dates to the
16 nation's beginning." And then, finally, Windsor says,
17 on 2692, "The State's power in defining the marital
18 relation is of central relevance in this case, quite
19 apart from the principles of federalism."
20 And, in that case, New York gave a new definition
21 of marriage to include same-sex couples. Windsor
22 respects the state's authority and autonomy to do so.

208

23 What the problem was is not whether that was
24 constitutional or not within the state, but when a state
25 ultimately chooses to change the definition of marriage
1-888-311-4240
WWW.USLEGALSUPPORT.COM
36
1 in this case, whether the federal government could
2 ultimately prohibit the state from giving that kind of
3 classification to its own citizens, and the Supreme
4 Court said that it could not.
5 But, within that same Supreme Court decision, it
6 clearly, multiple times, said that it is the sovereignty
7 and the very central power of the state to not just
8 regulate marriage, but to define the definition of
9 marriage. Windsor gives the authority for states to do
10 so and Windsor did not affect the states' rights to do
11 so. That's why it didn't implicate Baker vs. Nelson,
12 because Baker vs. Nelson was not relevant in that
13 particular context.
14 THE COURT: But, in its dicta, doesn't it attack
15 the motivation for DOMA?
16 MR. STAVER: It attacked the motivation for the
17 Federal Defense of Marriage Act, not for state marriage
18 laws that define marriage. Because, in that particular
19 case, they cited some congressional testimony or
20 congressional legislative history with respect to some
21 of the legislators when they passed or voted upon
DOMA
22 as to what their motivation was. We don't have that
23 here in this particular case. We don't have that.
24 THE COURT: But, didn't it attack the definition of
25 marriage under DOMA as violating the constitution?
1-888-311-4240
WWW.USLEGALSUPPORT.COM

37

1 MR. STAVER: No. It attacked only the federal
2 government's prohibition of not recognizing a state's
3 definition of marriage and left intact the state's
4 right, as a sovereign state, to define the definition of
5 marriage, multiple times. And, those were just examples
6 of quotes from Windsor.
7 THE COURT: Well, at minimum, it strongly
8 criticized the definition that --
9 MR. STAVER: It strongly --
10 THE COURT: It criticized the definition of
11 marriage under DOMA.
12 MR. STAVER: It criticized the definition of
13 marriage because of the reason why the 1996 -- I think I
14 may have said 2006, it was 1996 -- legislature, Congress
15 ultimately made statements as to their motivation. But,
16 it didn't criticize the definition of marriage, in
17 general, and certainly allowed states to have their own
18 sovereignty in defining marriage.
19 Just not long ago, Justice Kennedy, who wrote
20 Windsor, also, I believe, was the author of the Schuette
21 case, a Supreme Court decision. And in that particular
22 case, that dealt with affirmative action in Michigan.
23 And, I'd like to just read a paragraph in that because,
24 putting Schuette together with Windsor, Windsor being
25 that states have the right to define marriage and

38

1 Schuette ultimately respected the definition of or the
2 voter's rights in Michigan.
3 It says, "Were the court to rule that the question
4 addressed by Michigan voters is too sensitive or complex
5 to be within the grasp of the electorate or that the

6 policies at issue remain too delicate to be resolved
7 save by university officials or faculties acting at some
8 or removed from any media or public scrutiny and
9 control, or that these matters are so arcane that the
10 electorate's power must be limited because the people
11 cannot prudently exercise that power even after a full
12 debate, that holding would be an unprecedented
13 restriction on the exercise of a fundamental right held,
14 not just by one person, but by all in common. It is the
15 right to speak and debate and learn and then, as a
16 matter of political will, to act through a lawful
17 electoral process."
18 That's at page 1637 of the Supreme Court's decision
19 in Schuette. And, that was dealing with the passage of
20 the state law or state referendum on affirmative action
21 where the state did not want to have affirmative action.
22 It was challenged as a violation of equal protection
23 law. And, Kennedy, writing the majority opinion, says
24 that that is the sovereignty of the state to be able to
25 do that and engage in that political will.
1-888-311-4240
WWW.USLEGALSUPPORT.COM
39
1 That's what Florida did in 2008, and even before
2 that through the legislative process in '97 and '77, and
3 all the way back to the very beginning.
4 So, the Supreme Court of the United States gives
5 the right of the people to be able to have that kind of
6 sovereignty. But, specifically, even though it is still
7 subject to federal constitutional review, Windsor
8 specifically and multiple times, states that it is the
9 sovereignty of a state to define marriage.
10 Chief Justice John Roberts, in his opinion in the
11 Windsor case, specifically said, this case is not about

12 same-sex marriage with regards to the marriage laws
13 within the states.
14 Moving on from there to Baker, before I go to the
15 rational basis, Baker vs. Nelson is still the law of the
16 land and whether we or anyone believes that a legal
17 precedent has changed or that the climate has changed or
18 people opinions have changed, notwithstanding, there's
19 only one court in the country that has the right to say
20 so and that is the court that issued the opinion, the
21 United States Supreme Court.
22 I know that the plaintiffs had indicated, why is
23 Baker such a problematic case for us, was mentioned
24 during the opening argument. I can answer that very
25 simply, because it's controlling precedent. It is a

40

1 problematic case for them and the State has raised Baker
2 vs. Nelson.
3 In fact, in the Wilson vs. Ake case, in the Middle
4 District of Florida, the Florida, in 2005, the Federal
5 District Court specifically said that Baker vs. Nelson
6 is still controlling. There's multiple other -- it
7 says, quote, "Baker vs. Nelson is binding precedent upon
8 this court."
9 In 2004, 2005, there were five same-sex marriage
10 cases filed in Florida. That was before the Marriage
11 Protection Amendment. All of those cases were
12 dismissed. Baker vs. Nelson was cited specifically in
13 the Wilson case as binding precedent as the reason for
14 the dismissal.
15 And, when the Supreme Court issues a dismissal, as
16 it did in Baker vs. Nelson, it is a decision on the

17 merits and there's multiple Supreme Court cases that
18 say, until and unless -- first of all, that it's a
19 decision on the merits and it's binding precedent.
20 And, secondly, until and unless the Supreme Court
21 changes that, you can't even consider by implication
22 because of a changed precedent or a change of a society
23 that it's no longer binding. The only court that has
24 the province and the ability to do that is the court
25 that issued it.
1-888-311-4240
WWW.USLEGALSUPPORT.COM
41
1 Now, the Plaintiffs say that Baker vs. Nelson is no
2 longer binding. There is no case that says that it's no
3 longer binding from the Supreme Court. It's never
4 suggested it. If Baker were no longer binding, if it
5 had some erosion of its underlying principles, then
6 clearly the decision in Windsor, just last year, would
7 have said so, and didn't mention it at all, because it
8 is continuing to be binding.
9 Irrespective of what Minnesota does, whether they
10 pass same-sex marriage or have marriage as the union of
11 one man and one woman, that doesn't make any
difference
12 as to whether that case, arising out of Minnesota,
13 changes for the rest of the country. Because Minnesota
14 decides to go in a different direction or stay in the
15 same direction, it's irrelevant. It's a decision, not
16 of Minnesota, it's a decision from the United States
17 Supreme Court. So, jurisdictionally, this case should
18 fall on that argument alone.
19 Before 2013, there were about 50 marriage cases
20 around the country. We were involved in litigating on
21 most of those cases. Not all. Some of them mentioned

22 Baker, but many of them didn't mention Baker. Some of
23 them just didn't even know that Baker existed, because
24 it wasn't in the briefing, apparently. But, of those
25 cases, when you look at the history of same-sex

1-888-311-4240
WWW.USLEGALSUPPORT.COM

42

1 marriage, the first time that we ever had same-sex
2 marriage in the entire world was in 2000, and that was
3 in the Netherlands, and they had same-sex civil unions.
4 It wasn't quite marriage, but it was a civil union. The
5 first time we ever had it in the United States was in
6 Massachusetts when the decision in 2003 became effective
7 in 2004.
8 So, we're into this experiment only, in the United
9 States, ten years, and, in world history, 14 years. The
10 Greeks, even though they may have been more permissive
11 in terms of human sexuality, never adopted same-sex
12 marriage. So, in world history, we're into this 14
13 years, and, in the United States, only ten years.
14 Consequently, what we have here between 2004 and
15 2013, are about 50 cases that happened. Historically,
16 if you look at some of these challenges, a couple of
17 them happened in the 70s, and it really began in 2004,
18 in San Francisco, when Mayor Gavin issued, began to
19 issue same-sex marriage licenses there in that city.
20 From then until 2013, about 50-plus marriage cases.
21 And, except for the Massachusetts Supreme Judicial
22 Court in 2003, that became effective in 2004, and except
23 for the federal judge in California in the Proposition 8
24 case, these cases consistently went with the state's
25 definition of marriage, whether it's in a marriage

1 amendment or whether it is in a state statute or
2 inherent within the law. In some particular cases, it
3 wasn't specific DOMA legislative or initiative, it was
4 inherent within the law.
5 Case after case, they upheld these. Many of them
6 cited Baker vs. Nelson as controlling precedent. But,
7 all of the cases looked at rational basis. It concluded
8 that the state clearly had rational basis and that that
9 was the standard of review. From two-thousand-and --
10 THE COURT: Are you familiar with De Leon vs. Perry
11 from the Western District of Texas?
12 MR. STAVER: Yes.
13 THE COURT: And, how they dealt with Baker?
14 MR. STAVER: I'm familiar with how some of these
15 courts, since two-thousand-and --
16 THE COURT: And, Texas law is very similar to
17 Florida law, correct, that is in question?
18 MR. STAVER: It's similar. It's not the same, but
19 it's similar.
20 THE COURT: Very similar.
21 MR. STAVER: Yeah. In terms of how some of the
22 cases since 2013 have dealt with Baker, I submit that
23 they over-read anything from the Supreme Court,
because
24 the Supreme Court has made one pronouncement and
that's
25 Baker vs. Nelson. They have not done anything in

1 Lawrence vs. Texas, nothing in Roman, nothing more

2 particularly in Windsor, to suggest that the Supreme

3 Court is going in a different direction.

4 Irrespective of what any court has suggested Baker

5 may or may not be binding precedent, that's the province

6 of the United States Supreme Court. It is still binding

7 precedent. And, if we have a decision only a year ago

8 in the Windsor case that never even suggested that Baker

9 -- it didn't even refer to Baker as suspect, that is

10 still binding precedent. They would have -- in fact, in

11 the lower court, they did refer to Baker and the Supreme

12 Court did not address Baker when it came up to the

13 United States Supreme Court. So, Baker is still binding

14 precedent and it's still binding precedent on this

15 Court, as well.

16 THE COURT: I understand your argument. Would you

17 please address now, setting aside the United States

18 Constitution, Florida Constitution.

19 MR. STAVER: Yes, sure.

20 THE COURT: Which provides more protection.

21 MR. STAVER: Yes. Two different arguments on that.

22 First of all, only five days ago, I think it was July

23 the 2nd, in response to the State of Florida's motion in

24 memorandum on the Baker vs. Nelson issue, the Plaintiffs

25 raised the Article I, Section 23, Florida Right to

1-888-311-4240

WWW.USLEGALSUPPORT.COM

45

1 Privacy that was passed in the 1980s.

2 We're at summary judgment and that was never raised

3 in the complaint. In fact, the only constitutional

4 provision in the count that was raised in the complaint

5 was the United States Constitution, which we've already

6 addressed Baker and Windsor and Schuette and so forth.

7 So, first, from a procedural standpoint, it's too
8 late to raise a brand new constitutional provision as a
9 basis for relief when no one has had the opportunities
10 to submit opposing briefs on the issue. That's number
11 one and that would be basic.
12 But, more particularly, even if it were before the
13 Court today, Article I, Section 23, cannot trump a
14 subsequent constitutional amendment in the same
Article.
15 Article I, Section 23, whatever it means with regards to
16 the right of privacy and how broad it may be in any
17 other particular case, one thing clearly it does not
18 mean is that it does not apply to give a right to same-
19 sex marriage. It cannot, by virtue of the fact that
20 Article I, Section 27, passed by the voters, amended the
21 constitution in 2008, and whatever it could have been
22 interpreted to apply to, which it never was before 2008,
23 it cannot now be interpreted to apply to a right to
24 same-sex marriage.
25 THE COURT: So, are you saying that the amendment
1-888-311-4240
WWW.USLEGALSUPPORT.COM
46
1 then bypasses any scrutiny under the Florida
2 Constitution?
3 MR. STAVER: Yes. The Article I, Section 23, in
4 itself, says that in -- as it relates to this issue of
5 marriage, it is constitutional within our constitution
6 and there cannot be any other constitutional provision
7 in the state constitution that contradicts that.
8 THE COURT: Doesn't that lead to the possibility of
9 contradiction in the constitution --
10 MR. STAVER: The only time that it --
11 THE COURT: -- between sections?

12 MR. STAVER: The only time it could be a
13 contradiction is if it was an amendment to a previous
14 statute.
15 Now, the Plaintiffs could have an argument if it
16 was reversed; if the Florida Marriage Protection Act was
17 passed in 1980 and then the Right to Privacy Amendment
18 was passed in 2008. Then, they might have an argument
19 to that effect that it controls by giving a greater
20 right to privacy. But, in the sequence in which it
21 happened with 1980 or so being the Article I, Section
22 23, 2008 being Article I, Section 27, specifically in
23 that section of enumerating individual liberties and
24 rights and so forth, stating that marriage is the union
25 of a man and a woman and no state or agency can

1-888-311-4240
WWW.USLEGALSUPPORT.COM

47

1 recognize anything to the contrary, whatever Article I,
2 Section 23 [sic] means in any other context, it cannot
3 mean, by virtue of that subsequently passed amendment,
4 that it applies to same-sex marriage.
5 So, on the merits, even if it were before the
6 Court, it fails, just like a subsequent adopted statute.
7 If the law is, in one particular section of the statute,
8 exists, and the legislature adopts a subsequent law that
9 has some kind of conflict, it's presumed that they knew
10 that that was there and, therefore, even though it may
11 not directly reference it, it is an amendment or it's an
12 exception to whatever it was before, and that's exactly
13 what we have here in Article I.
14 It's not in a different article, it's in the exact
15 same article. It's only removed by a few sections in
16 the article. So, on the merits, that particular

17 argument fails.

18 Plus, even before, there's never been a -- cases,

19 in fact, as I was mentioning before, in 2005, there were

20 about five cases filed against the Florida marriage laws

21 before the 2008 marriage amendment. None of those

22 courts ultimately ruled Article I, Section 23, gives a

23 right to same-sex marriage.

24 Are there any other questions on that, Your Honor?

25 THE COURT: I do not have any. Thank you.

1-888-311-4240

WWW.USLEGALSUPPORT.COM

48

1 MR. STAVER: Okay. Let me just go on and wrap up

2 my argument here in just a few moments.

3 Windsor gives the authority to the states to

4 definitely define marriage. Schuette gives the

5 authority to states to have a referendum within 2013,

6 2014. Article I, Section 23, clearly doesn't apply for

7 the reasons I've mentioned. And, Baker vs. Nelson does

8 apply. We respect that that should end the discussion.

9 But, going back to how I began with regards to the

10 burden on the Plaintiff, the Plaintiff has the burden of

11 proving that there's no disputes in the material facts.

12 It has to be a conclusive proof so that anyone looking

13 at it would conclusively agree with the Plaintiffs, and

14 that simply hasn't been happening, it simply hasn't

15 happened. They also have to negate every rational

16 basis.

17 With regards to rational basis, this Court

18 mentioned X.X.G. X.X.G. was an adoption case that began

19 here in the Keys. The D.M.T. case actually cites X.X.G.

20 for the proposition that rational basis applies because

21 sexual orientation is not the determinate of or

22 constitute a protected class.

23 But, D.M.T. also cites X.X.G. one more time on

24 pages 343 and 344. And, in that particular case, it

25 uses it for the analogy that the parties in that case

49

1 agree that gay people and heterosexuals make equally-

2 good parents. Then it goes on, likewise, in this case,

3 the D.M.T. case, no party and no Amicus Curiae has

4 advanced the argument that either T.M.H. or, for that

5 matter, D.M.T. is unfit to be a parent.

6 That X.X.G. case was in 2010. Since then, the

7 numerous studies that have come out, and one of those is

8 one that we presented before the Court, it's the study

9 by Mark Regnerus. And, contrary to the Plaintiffs'

10 statement that he's been rejected by his own university,

11 that's just simply not the case.

12 Mark Regnerus did a peer-review study. It wasn't

13 something in which Mark just wrote an article and some

14 entity decided to publish it. This particular study

15 with regards to parenting was peer reviewed by other

16 people in the sociological arena and passed through that

17 peer review and was ultimately published two years after

18 the X.X.G. case, which was 2010. The Regnerus study was

19 2012.

20 And, Regnerus, as we cited in our brief beginning

21 on page 24, and we actually have the entire study before

22 the Court, one of the things that he found was that

23 children that are raised in the home with opposite

24 gender moms and dads do well on all of the different

25 measurable scales. Children raised by lesbians fared

WWW.USLEGALSUPPORT.COM
50
1 worse in educational attainment, family out of origin,
2 safety, security and it goes on through a whole list.
3 And then, also, those raised by gay fathers also
4 reported, and it goes through the entire litany of the
5 report; less education, lower scores on the family of
6 origin, safety, security, then it says, greater
7 depression and think that the current relationship is in
8 trouble.
9 And, he goes on to conclude by this that children
10 raised in a home with a mom and a dad that are male and
11 female fare better on all the different measurable
12 scales than children who are raised in a same-sex
13 household. Regnerus' study is not the first study to
14 show that. In fact, several studies, a huge sampling of
15 studies in Great Britain and also Holland and other
16 studies around the country, even Stacey and Biblarz who
17 were at the University of California, who support same-
18 sex marriage, have done studies and said that there are
19 differences between children who are raised in same-sex
20 households versus those who are raised in opposite-sex
21 households and it's different on all the different
22 measurable scales.
23 That goes back to the affidavit that John
24 Stemberger presented, that the purpose of the Florida
25 Marriage Protection Amendment, Article I, Section 27,
1-888-311-4240
WWW.USLEGALSUPPORT.COM
51
1 was to provide the best environment for children.
2 Children do best when they're raised in an environment
3 with mom and dad. And, those studies are coming out

4 more and more.

5 We're here on a significant issue of the

6 redefinition of marriage that goes far beyond just the

7 two people before this Court in terms of their

8 relationship with one another. To redefine marriage as

9 we're into this in the United States only ten years, has

10 huge consequential implications. To just simply remove

11 one gender from the family and say that we're going to

12 elevate this to the highest aspirational level of

13 marriage and put all of the laws and protections around

14 it, as a policy matter, that says that children don't

15 need moms and dads. As a policy matter, that dads are

16 irrelevant in the well being of young boys or young

17 girls; or, moms are irrelevant in the well being of

18 young boys or young girls. And, there's studies that

19 cannot just simply be brushed off, especially at this

20 stage of summary judgment, as though they don't matter.

21 Children do best as being raised in an environment

22 with opposite-sex parents and Florida is not unique in

23 having marriage as a union of one man and one woman.

24 The understanding of the marriage predates religion. It

25 wasn't created by any religion. It may be accepted by

1-888-311-4240

WWW.USLEGALSUPPORT.COM

52

1 various religions, strongly and whatever way. It may be

2 accepted by different governments and countries and

3 political entities. But, it predates all of that. It

4 predates any social compact. It predates any religion,

5 and for good reason. And, though the Plaintiffs want to

6 just simply brush off the procreation component, in the

7 best interests of children, with all due respect, that

8 is what we're dealing with in the redefinition of

9 marriage. It has huge implications, far beyond the
10 Plaintiffs in this case, to affect children and to
11 affect everyone around the country.
12 THE COURT: But, if children can still be adopted
13 by homosexuals and, in this case, if you are successful,
14 the amendment stands, those family units, although not
15 legally married, are going to remain intact. So, how
16 does that address the rational basis that you're saying
17 is the reason for this amendment?
18 MR. STAVER: Well, I think the --
19 THE COURT: I mean, the kids aren't going to be
20 removed from that environment.
21 MR. STAVER: No.
22 THE COURT: They can still adopt, they can still go
23 to a surrogate. There's different circumstances where
24 they can still have a family unit. So, how does this
25 amendment saying you cannot have same-sex marriage
1-888-311-4240
WWW.USLEGALSUPPORT.COM
53
1 address that?
2 MR. STAVER: I think the rational basis for this
3 amendment, and not just this amendment because there
are
4 other laws here that get challenged, as well, is what
5 has historically been part of marriage and that is
6 procreation and best interests of children. The best
7 interests of children. Not that children who are raised
8 in a single-parent household or in a same-sex household
9 are always going to be in a category that are not
10 performing as well, but as a policy matter, Florida has
11 the right and the voters affirmed that longstanding
12 understanding of marriage to be able to create an
13 environment in which it is the best interests of

14 children and that's what marriage does.
15 And, not only, even though there may be alternative
16 ways, artificial insemination, to procreate, still, it
17 comes from the male/female species. Marriage is the
18 joining together of a complementary nature of the sexes,
19 from which procreation occurs, the only way that
20 procreation can occur. Whether it's naturally or
21 artificially, it's the only way it can occur. Without
22 that, there is no future generation. And then, once the
23 generation is created, whether artificially or
24 naturally, the best environment. And, the studies back
25 up Florida's rational basis, as just one of many, shows
1-888-311-4240
WWW.USLEGALSUPPORT.COM
54
1 that children do best when they're raised in that
2 environment.
3 Steven Kurtzman [sic], and he is cited in our
4 brief, he looks at what happened in -- Steven Kurtz, I'm
5 sorry. Stanley Kurtz, "The End of Marriage in
6 Scandinavia," on page 17 of our brief, and Stanley Kurtz
7 did some sociological research in Scandinavia which
8 adopted same-sex civil unions in 2000, very similar to
9 marriage, although it didn't use the term at that time.
10 Marriage was already, at that time, in Scandinavia, in a
11 difficult situation.
12 And, Scandinavia has sort of been the bellwether
13 part of the world for marriage. What happens in
14 Scandinavia, oftentimes goes to Europe with regards to
15 marriage. It's just historically been that way. And
16 then, from there, comes to the United States.
17 In Scandinavia, they already had some difficulty
18 with marriages falling apart, not being lasting. And
19 then, in 2000, they adopted same-sex civil unions. When

20 that happened, he says that Scandinavian gay marriage
21 has driven home the message that marriage itself is
22 outdated, that virtually any family form, including out-
23 of-wedlock parenthood, is acceptable. He has much
24 other, many other words to say about that. But, one of
25 the things that we've seen in that 14-year experiment is
1-888-311-4240
WWW.USLEGALSUPPORT.COM
55
1 it didn't strengthen marriage. It actually caused the
2 further deterioration of marriage. And, when we start
3 to deteriorate marriage and that family unit, it has
4 economic consequences, as well, when those family units
5 disintegrate.
6 In fact, the Plaintiffs' argument with regard to
7 same-sex marriage has no boundaries. The Plaintiffs'
8 argument is not to just redefine marriage to include two
9 people of the same sex. The implications of that is if
10 you include two people of the same sex, then why can't
11 you have a person of opposite sex that also brings in a
12 same-sex partner to the marriage?
13 There is no logical or legal dividing line when you
14 cross the boundary of gender with regards to marriage
15 that ultimately prevents it going from there to polygamy
16 or, even in other cases, polyamory. And those arguments
17 are clearly being made in courts today as a result of
18 these marriage cases.
19 THE COURT: Well, there's a statute against
20 polygamy, so that --
21 MR. STAVER: Well, there's a statute against
22 polygamy, but there's also a constitutional amendment
23 against same-sex marriage. And, if all of that goes, if
24 all of that goes and gender is no longer relevant to the

25 marriage relationship, then there is no legal reason to

56

1 not extend it beyond, and that's exactly what's
2 happening in other places around the country.
3 We presented other rational bases in addition to
4 the complementary nature of the sex and procreation, the
5 best interests of children, the health and well being.
6 We've put in our brief a lot of information regarding
7 the health and well being of the individuals involved
8 themselves as a rational basis. But, the only rational
9 basis that's, I think, necessary is what's already been
10 presented and the State -- or, the Plaintiff has not
11 carried the burden to negate that as a rational basis.
12 They can't just simply come here and argue, number
13 one, that there's animus, when they have no evidence of
14 it. And, when the only contrary information is that it
15 wasn't passed because of hatred or animus or bigotry,
16 it's actually the opposite. And, they can't come here
17 and say that there's no rational basis with regards to
18 the best interests of children when they've presented no
19 information regarding that. And, yet, the studies that
20 are there contradict what the Plaintiffs have stated.
21 So, for the reasons that we've presented that this
22 case is not ripe for summary judgment and Plaintiffs
23 have not met their burden in bringing this case to
24 summary judgment, that Windsor and Schuette allow the
25 State to define marriage, and that Baker vs. Nelson

57

1 controls, and Article I, Section 23 is not before the

2 Court. And, even if it were, it fails on the merits and
3 the fact that there's multiple rational basis for these
4 laws. We respectfully request this Court to deny the
5 Plaintiffs relief.
6 THE COURT: Thank you. Mr. Saunders and State of
7 Florida, is there a dispute as to the underlying facts
8 of this case, as the Defendants in this case?
9 MR. SAUNDERS: No, Your Honor.
10 MR. TANENBAUM: No, Your Honor.
11 THE COURT: Okay. Thank you.
12 Counsel for the Plaintiff.
13 MS. VIGIL-FARINAS: Well, Judge, the sky is
14 falling. We're going to become a polygamous state, our
15 children are going to get destroyed, on and on and on.
16 Chicken Little has his own opinions, I guess.
17 All right. Your Honor, this case is not about
18 whether marriage between same-sex couples are
consistent
19 or inconsistent with the teachings of a particular
20 religion, whether such marriages are moral or immoral
or
21 whether they are something that should be encouraged
or
22 discouraged. It is not even about whether the
23 plaintiffs in this case are as capable as opposite-sex
24 couples of maintaining a committed and loving
25 relationship or raising a family. It's already been
1-888-311-4240
WWW.USLEGALSUPPORT.COM
58
1 established that they can raise a family.
2 Quite simply, this case is about liberty and
3 equality, the two cornerstones of the rights protected
4 by the U.S. Constitution. Now, ironically, Amicus

5 claims that he represents PULSE, People United,

6 something, something for Equality, to Lead the Struggle

7 for Equality. I don't really get that, but that's

8 neither here nor there.

9 What has to fall, Judge, is not the sky. What has

10 to fall is these laws that discriminate against a

11 portion of our society. They're wrong. And sometimes,

12 a decision isn't the easiest decision, it's the right

13 decision. And, these laws are wrong. There is no proof

14 at all, this brief presented by Amicus -- now, I

15 appreciate the fact that he feels that the State of

16 Florida isn't doing their job and that they're not

17 saying that we don't have a motion for summary
judgment

18 proper before this Court, and all these other

19 allegations that he's making, which he has no standing

20 to make. I appreciate that. But, the crux of this

21 manifesto, written by the Amicus, is horrible. There's

22 no legal argument here. There are no facts in here.

23 It's a manifesto of bigotry. That's all it is.

24 Now, I want to read one paragraph to this Court

25 which I have read myself 16 times and it stuns me every

1 time I read it. Now, this is their rationalization as

2 to why this ban should be allowed.

3 "Anal intercourse is a sine qua non of sex for many

4 gay men, yet human physiology makes it clear that the

5 body was not designed to accommodate this activity. The

6 rectum is significantly different from the vagina with

7 regard to suitability for penetration by the penis. The

8 vagina has natural lubricants and is supported by a

9 network of muscles." Blah, blah, blah. "Consequently,

10 anal intercourse leads to a leakage of fecal material
11 that could easily become chronic."
12 That's a rational reason, a legal reason, or is it
13 just bigotry? I'm embarrassed. I'm embarrassed to have
14 a member of the Bar write something like this as an
15 excuse to support the bigotry of the voters of Florida.
16 Because, in his mind, this Court should allow mob rule.
17 If the majority, the ones that have the most money, the
18 ones that have the most position, don't like a certain
19 segment of society, like our friends over here, they get
20 to rule and you don't get to even evaluate whether or
21 not it's constitutional. So, why are you here? Why are
22 any of the courts here?
23 What would this state be like if we allowed mob
24 rule? Today, it's against Aaron and tomorrow it could
25 be against me. I wasn't born here. They need to get
1-888-311-4240
WWW.USLEGALSUPPORT.COM
60
1 out of peoples' bedrooms.
2 Now, let me tell you some facts. These laws in
3 that Amendment 27 are discriminatory. The fundamental
4 right to marry under the Due Process Clause encompasses
5 the rights of individuals to marry someone of the same
6 sex. There is no asterisk besides, you know, Article 14
7 saying it doesn't apply to that -- Amendment 14, I
8 apologize. There is none. It applies to everyone
9 equally.
10 The marriage amendment and the relevant statutes
11 were subject to heightened scrutiny. Why? Because it
12 applies to equal protection claims involving sexual
13 orientation discrimination. Despite what the Amicus
14 says, it does apply. We are at a heightened scrutiny.

15 And, even if we weren't in a heightened scrutiny, let's
16 assume the worse case scenario for us, it's a rational
17 basis test. Outside of all of these alleged studies,
18 where is the rational basis?
19 This Court has not heard one good reason why you
20 should not tell the State of Florida, you can't do this.
21 They have as many rights as we do. And, the argument -
-
22 first of all, we're not in Scandinavia, we're here. And
23 second of all, the argument that Scandinavia is having
24 problems with marriages falling apart; seriously? 57
25 percent of first marriages in this country fall apart,

1-888-311-4240
WWW.USLEGALSUPPORT.COM
61

1 64 percent of second marriages and 72 percent of third
2 marriages, and they're asking for the right to be as
3 miserable as all the rest of us are.
4 And, how allowing gay couples to marry affects
5 heterosexual couples, the population of the world is
6 going to diminish? How does one thing affect the other?
7 What do you care who someone loves? How is it going to
8 keep anyone from getting married who is heterosexual?
9 And, having kids; is that what we're put on this planet
10 for? Some of us, if we'd known, we would have stuck
11 with doggies.
12 So, you can't sit here and tell me, unless you are
13 going to put some kind of requirement on a marriage
14 license that everyone who applies for a marriage license
15 must be able to procreate children. Their argument is
16 ridiculous. It's ridiculous. There is no legitimate
17 reason, but for bigotry. There is no legitimate reason,
18 but for discrimination.
19 THE COURT: Would you address Baker?

20 MS. VIGIL-FARINAS: Oh, God, I'm so sick of Baker.
21 Yes, I'll address Baker.
22 Judge, every court in the past, easy, eight or nine
23 years, has said that Baker is dead letter. It's done.
24 I'm going to cite to you from a case which I thought was
25 an extraordinary opinion from the United States District

62

1 Court in Wisconsin. And, they, I guess, are also very
2 tired of having people talk about Baker.
3 It seems to me like they have nothing else to argue
4 but Baker and just want to resurrect it every time
5 there's an argument. Baker is dead. And, this court
6 says, the "The rule for summary affirmances," which is
7 what we had -- and it's a summary dismissal, first of
8 all, in Baker. It wasn't an opinion. It was a summary
9 dismissal. It was not based on the merits of the case.
10 "The rule of summary affirmances and dismissals is
11 not so clear cut. Those orders are not the same
12 precedential value as would be an opinion of the Supreme
13 Court treating the question on the merits. A summary
14 dismissal is no longer controlling when the trial
15 developments indicate that the court would take a
16 different view now. They would be an understatement to
17 say the Supreme Court's jurisprudence on issues similar
18 to those raised in Baker have developed substantially
19 since 1972. At the time, few courts had addressed any
20 issues relating to the constitutional rights of gay
21 persons. Favorable decisions were even less frequent."
22 As a matter of fact, in 1967, in Boutilier vs.
23 Immigration and Naturalization Service, gay

homosexual
24 individuals were denied entry into the United States
25 because it was assumed that their homosexuality was a

63

1 psychopathic personality. Thank God we've come a little
2 bit further than that. Yet, they keep wanting to go
3 back to that era. They want to keep going back to the
4 era where the gay people are considered they need to be
5 in a straightjacket in the hospital It's done. It was
6 42 years ago. Get over it.
7 THE COURT: What about the argument that, in your
8 complaint, the argument that you've -- or, you brought
9 forward today about the Florida Constitution that is not
10 in your complaint?
11 MS. VIGIL-FARINAS: He has no standing to argue
12 what the State didn't argue. Again, I appreciate him
13 wanting to litigate for the State, but it's not his
14 position.
15 And, Judge, as these cases progress, the State came
16 in at the last minute because it was the politically
17 necessary thing to do. Waited four months before even
18 making an appearance. They're not arguing it. I don't
19 think anyone can justifiably argue that these laws and
20 this amendment are constitutional, because they're not.
21 Do you know how much hate mail we've gotten? It's
22 disgusting. That you feel that you have the right to
23 tell someone who you can and can't love and you who
24 can't be with is disgusting. Yet, the State of Florida
25 allows murderers in jail to get married. Right? And,

64

1 some of them are lucky enough to have visits and
2 procreate. But, we won't let two decent human beings
3 who love each other get married? We'll let a rapist get
4 married. We'll let a pedophile get married.
5 And, what's the big deal of marriage? Frankly, I
6 don't even know. It's a society thing. But, the bottom
7 line is they have the right to it. They have a right to
8 the dignity of saying, I love him, he loves me, and
9 we're married. And, it does give them a place in
10 society. It validates who they are and who they love.
11 Now, all the other courts in the past, I don't
12 know, six months or so, have been falling like dominoes.
13 Not because the litigation has been so fantastic, but
14 because it's the right thing to do. And, even outside
15 the four walls of Monroe County, there are some rational
16 people out there and there are considerate people out
17 there. And, again, the questions that everyone has to
18 ask each other; how does it affect you? How does it
19 affect you? What do you care?
20 THE COURT: But, the legal question is a rational
21 basis, at minimum.
22 MS. VIGIL-FARINAS: The legal question is high
23 scrutiny. But, yes, we can go for rational basis,
24 because there is none. It doesn't matter. We can go to
25 the highest level of standard we can go to the lowest.
1-888-311-4240
WWW.USLEGALSUPPORT.COM
65
1 In the realm of standards for this particular situation,
2 there's nothing.
3 What has the State presented to you? I'm not even
4 going to the Amicus because I was just disgusted by the

5 entire thing.

6 THE COURT: All right. But, --

7 MS. VIGIL-FARINAS: But, what has the State

8 presented to you? We voted it in, you need to respect

9 that. Sure, you need to respect it, but you certainly

10 have the right to find out whether or not it's a

11 constitutional thing. Whether or not people are being

12 deprived of rights that are fundamentally theirs,

13 because, today it's them, tomorrow it's somebody else.

14 THE COURT: Understood.

15 MS. VIGIL-FARINAS: Thank you, Judge.

16 THE COURT: Thank you. Thank you all. Good

17 morning, have a good morning.

18 (The proceeding was concluded at 11:10 a.m.)

19

20

21

22

23

24

25

1-888-311-4240

WWW.USLEGALSUPPORT.COM

66

CERTIFICATE OF REPORTER

STATE OF FLORIDA)

COUNTY OF MONROE)

I, Suzanne Ex, Certified Verbatim Reporter and

Florida Professional Reporter, do HEREBY CERTIFY

that I was

authorized to and did report the foregoing proceedings;

and

that the transcript, pages 1 through 65 are a true and

correct record of my notes.

I further certify that I am not a relative,
employee, attorney, or counsel of any of the parties, nor am
I a relative or employee of any of the parties' attorneys or
counsel connected with the action, nor am I financially
interested in the action.
Dated this 21st day of July, 2014.

Suzanne Ex, FPR, CVR-M
Florida Professional Reporter
Certified Verbatim Reporter-Master

. .

1-888-311-4240
WWW.USLEGALSUPPORT.COM

JUDGE GARCIA'S RULING ON HUNTSMAN V HEAVILIN

IN THE CIRCUIT COURT SIXTEENTH JUDICIAL CIRCUIT
IN AND FOR MONROE COUNTY, FLORIDA
AARON R. HUNTSMAN, et aI.,

Plaintiffs,

vs.

AMY HEAVILIN, as Clerk of the Courts
of Monroe County, Florida, in her official
capacity,

Defendant,

and

STATE OF FLORIDA,

Intervenor-Defendant.

/

CASE NO.: 2014-CA-30S-K
ORDER ON PLAINTIFF'S MOTION FOR SUMMARY JUDGMENT

The court having considered the Plaintiffs' verified complaint, the Plaintiff's motion for summary judgment and memorandum in support, the Declaration of Aaron R. Huntsman and William Lee Jones, the State of Florida's memorandum of law in opposition, the memorandum of law of Amici Curiae Florida Family Action, Inc. "FDL", and People United to Lead the Struggle for Equality Inc. "PULSE", in opposition to Plaintiffs' motion for summary judgment and the oral arguments held on July 7, 2014. The court makes the following findings:

Summary Judgment

Summary judgment shall only be granted when the moving party establishes conclusively the absence of any genuine issue of material fact. Moore v. Morris, 475 So.2d 666, (Fla. 1985). In the instant matter, the plaintiffs and the defendants have stipulated that there are no disputed facts that would prevent a ruling on plaintiffs' motion for summary judgment. However, Amici Curiae (FDL and PULSE) take the position that there are disputed facts that would prevent a granting of plaintiff's motion. Amici Curiae do not have standing to raise issues that have not been raised by the parties. Acton II v. Ft. Lauderdale Hospital, 418 So.2d 1099

Page 1 of **14**

(1st DCA 1982). Therefore, the court accepts the stipulation by the parties that there are no disputed facts that would prevent a ruling on plaintiff's motion for summary judgment.

Undisputed Facts

On April 1, 2014, the plaintiffs, a same-sex couple residing in Key West, Florida, applied and were denied a marriage license by the Clerk of the Court of Monroe County. The Clerk's denial was based on Florida law that required one of the applicants to be male and the other female; thereby, excluding same-sex couples from being married. The plaintiffs seek to publicly and officially have their eleven year relationship recognized and legitimized under Florida law. They seek to have their relationship accorded the dignity, respect and security as the relationships of other married couples in the State of Florida. In 2008, the voters of the State of Florida unequivocally voted in favor of an amendment to the Florida Constitution defining marriage, the Florida Marriage Protection Act (FMPA). The voter's intent is codified in Article I, Section 27 of the Florida Constitution.

Florida Laws at Issue

Florida Constitution Article I, Section 27 states: "Inasmuch as marriage is the legal union of only one man and one woman as husband and wife, no other legal union that is treated as marriage or the substantial equivalent thereof shall be valid or recognized," Florida Statute 741.04(1) forbids the issuance of a marriage license unless one party is male and the other female. Florida Statute 741.212(1) states that same-sex marriages from other states will not be recognized by the State of Florida.

Page 2 of 14

Issues

The plaintiffs hereby petition the court to find the above laws unconstitutional as violative of the Equal Protection and the Due Process Clause of the Fourteenth Amendment of the United States of America. The State of Florida takes the position that Article I, Section 27 of the Florida Constitution as enacted by Florida voters does not implicate Due Process or the Equal Protection Clause of the Fourteenth Amendment, citing to Baker v. Nelson, 409 U.S. 810 (1972). The state argues that under Baker v. Nelson, Article I, Section 27 is exempt from any constitutional scrutiny by any court in the United States until the United States Supreme Court overturns its decision in Baker v. Nelson. Until that time, a state's definition of marriage is not subject to judicial review on constitutional grounds because the regulation of marriage is exclusively the province of the state. Sosna v. Iowa, 419 U.s. 393 (1975). In the alternative, the State of Florida takes the position that if there is going to be constitutional scrutiny of Article I, Section 27, then the standard to be applied is the "Rational Basis Standard." Under this standard the law in question is accorded a strong presumption of validity and must be upheld if any reasonable conceivable state of facts could provide a rational basis for the classification. Romer v. Evans, 517 U.s. 620 (1996). The Amici Curiae, like the State of Florida, also argue that the court is precluded by the United States Supreme Court opinion in Baker v. Nelson from addressing any constitutional challenge to Article I, Section 27 of the Florida Constitution. In the alternative, the Amici Curiae argue that if Article I, Section 27 is subject to constitutional scrutiny it must be under the lower "Rational Basis Standard".

Page 3 of 14

Analysis

A. Baker v. Nelson

The State of Florida and Amici Curiae contend that pursuant to the United States Supreme Court decision in Baker v. Nelson, the traditional definition of marriage does not implicate the Due Process or Equal Protection Clause of the Fourteenth Amendment, because it has been long held that the definition of marriage is the exclusive province of the states. Sosna v. Iowa, 419 U.S. 393 (1975)

In Baker v. Nelson, the Minnesota Supreme Court held

that a Minnesota law that limited marriage to opposite sex couples did not violate the Equal Protection or Due Process Clause of the Fourteenth Amendment. On appeal in 1972, the United States Supreme Court summarily dismissed the case, "for want of a substantial Federal Question," by implication leaving the definition of marriage to be exclusively a state issue. Summary dismissals are binding precedents on lower courts. However, summary dispositions may lose their precedential value and are no longer binding, "When doctrinal developments indicate otherwise." Hicks v. Mirabda, 422 U.S. 332 (1975). Baker was decided over 40 years ago. Since then, there have been substantial changes in societal views as well as subsequent changes in Federal and state case law. See Romero v. Evans, 517 u.s, 620 (1996); Lawrence v. Texas, 539 U.S. 558 (2003); U.S. v. Windsor, 133 S. Ct. 2675 (2013). These changes compel this court to conclude that Baker v. Nelson is no longer binding and the issue of same-sex marriage has now become a Federal question. This court joins other state and federal courts that have held that Baker is no longer binding on lower courts. See Whitewood v. Wolf, 2014 WL 2058105 (M.D. Penn.2014); Geiger v. Kitzhaber, 2014 WL 2054264 (D. Oregon 2014); Kitchen v. Herbert, 2014 WL2868044 (10th Cir. 2014); Bishop v. u.s, ex.ReI.Holder, 962 F.supp.2d. 1252 (N.D. Oklahoma 2014); DeBoer v.

Page 4 of14

Snyder, 973 F.2d. 757 (E.D. Michigan 2014); Bostic v.Rainey, 970 F.Supp.2d 456 (E.D. Virginia 2014).

B. Due Process Clause

The Fourteenth Amendment of the United States of

America states: "No State shall make or enforce any law which shall abridge the privileges or immunities of citizens of the United States, nor shall any State deprive any person of life, liberty or property without Due Process of law; nor deny to any person within its jurisdiction the equal protection of the law." Within the body of the Fourteenth Amendment is the Due Process Clause, which guarantees all citizens have certain "fundamental rights" and that citizens have a right to "liberty" from governmental intrusion and this right is to be guaranteed and protected by the United States Constitution. The right to liberty has been described by the United States Supreme Court as, "the right to define one's own concept of existence, of meaning, of the universe, and of the mystery of human life." See Planned Parenthood v. Casey, 505 U.S. 833 (1992).

Encompassed within the right to liberty is the fundamental right to marry. Maynard v. Hill, 125 U.S. 190 (1888). In Maynard, the Supreme Court characterized marriage as "the most important relation in life" and "the foundation of the family and of society, without which there would be neither civilization nor progress." There is no dispute by the parties that the right to marry is a fundamental right protected by the Fourteenth Amendment. The parting-of- the-ways occurs on whether the right to marry belongs to the individual and that individual's choice of spouse or whether the state has the authority to dictate one's choice in spouse to the opposite sex. The Supreme Court has cautioned that the Due Process Clause only "protects those fundamental rights and liberties which are, objectively, deeply rooted in this Nation's history and tradition ..." Washington v. Glucksberg, 521 U.S. 702 (1997). These deeply rooted traditions have come into conflict with the principles of the Constitution, and when that has occurred the long standing tradition has been extmquished by the Constitution. An example of popular traditions

failing a constitutional challenge was Virginia's law against interracial marriage. Virginia's antimiscegenation law was based on a long historical tradition held by many states that forbid interracial couples from marrying. The Supreme Court in Loving v. Virginia, 338 U.S. 1 (1967), held that Virginia's anti-miscegenation statute was unconstitutional as violative of both the Due Process and Equal Protection Clause of the Fourteenth Amendment. The Supreme Court held that the right to marry "resides with the individual and cannot be infringed by the State." The Supreme Court in Turner v. Safley, 482 U.S. 78 (1987), once again reaffirmed that the right to marry resided with the individual when the court struck down a Missouri regulation that prohibited inmates from marrying without the prior approval of the prison superintendent. The Supreme Court held that even an inmate who clearly had a reduced expectation of liberty, retain his right to marry. The Supreme Court stated that "Inmate marriages like other marriages are expressions of emotional support and public commitment. These elements are a significant aspect of marital relationships...Taken together, we conclude that these elements are sufficient to form a constitutionally protected marital relationship in the prison contexts." In Lawrence v. Texas, 539 U.S. 558 (2003), the Supreme Court stated, "Had those who drew and ratified the Due Process Clauses of the Fifth Amendment or the Fourteenth Amendment known the components of liberty in its manifold possibilities, they may have been more specific. They did not presume to have this insight. **They knew times can blind us to certain truths**

and later generations can see that laws once thought necessary and proper in fact serve only to oppress. As the Constitution endures, persons in every generation can invoke its principles in their own search for greater freedom." (Emphasis added) This court concludes that a citizen's right to marry is a fundamental right that belongs to the individual. The right these plaintiffs seek is not a new right, but is a right that these individuals have always been guaranteed by the United States Constitution. Societal norms and traditions have kept same-sex couples from marrying, like it kept women from voting until 1920 and forbid interracial marriage until 1967.

Page 6 of 14

The Supreme Court in Lawrence explained that every generation defines its own freedom and that our present laws may be judged by future generations as oppressive and obviously unconstitutional. The same way we now look at laws that forbade interracial marriages, or excluded homosexuals from entering the country, or kept women from voting, or kept black children from going to school with white children or that the U.S. imprisoned JapaneseAmericans, on U.s. soil, in camps during WWII. When these laws were in effect, they were supported by society as being reflective of our traditions and morals at the time. Only when those not in power, challenged the constitutionality of those laws were they overturned by the courts regardless of the law's popularity and years of tradition. "One's right to life, liberty, and property, to free speech, a free press, freedom of worship and assembly, and other **fundamental rights may not be submitted to vote; they depend on the outcome of no elections."** W.

Virginia State Bd. Of Educ. v. Barnette, 319 U.S. 624 (1943). (Emphasis Added). This court holds that the fundamental right to marry belongs to the individual and is protected by the Due Process Clause of the Fourteenth Amendment to the United States Constitution and that right encompasses the right to marry a person of one's own sex. Thus Article I, Section 27 of the Florida Constitution and Florida Statute 741.04(1) are unconstitutional.

C. Equal Protection Clause

The Equal Protection Clause of the Fourteenth Amendment commands that no state shall deny to any person within its jurisdiction the equal protection of the law. The Constitution "neither knows nor tolerates classes among its citizens." Plessy v. Ferguson, 163 U.S.537 (1896)

.

When faced with an Equal Protection claim, the court must first determine whether to apply strict scrutiny, intermediate scrutiny or the rational basis standard. U.S. v. Virginia, 518 U.S. 515 (1996). The rational basis standard is the least strict or easiest to over-come by the

Page 7 of 14

government. Under the rational basis review, a classification will be upheld as long as there is a rational relationship between the disparity of treatment and some legitimate government purpose. Heller v. Doe, 509 U.S. 312 (1993). A law will not survive rational basis unless there is a legitimate government purpose for the law and the discrimination bears a rational relationship to achieve that purpose. City of Cleburne v. Cleburne living Center, 105 S. Ct. 3249 (1985). The plaintiffs have the burden of proving either that there is no legitimate purpose for the law or that the means chosen to effectuate that legitimate purpose are not rationally related to that purpose. Rational basis while deferential to the state, if the law exhibits a desire to harm a politically unpopular group the Supreme Court has applied "a more searching form of rational basis to strike down such laws under the Equal Protection Clause." See Lawrence v. Texas, 539 U.S. 588 (2003). Where a court suspects animus towards a disadvantaged group a more meaningful level of review is warranted. Several federal courts have used this heightened rational basis test or rational basis test with "teeth." See City of Cleburne v. Cleburne Living center, 105 S. Ct. 3249 (1985); Dept. of Agriculture v. Moreno, 413 U.S. 528 (1973); and most recently u.s. v. Windsor, 133 S. Ct. 2675 (2013). In Windsor, the Supreme Court found animus when it held that the principle of the Federal Defense of Marriage Act (DOMA) violated the Equal Protection guarantee because the "purpose and practical effect of the law... [was] to impose a disadvantage, a separate status, and so a stigma upon all who enter into a same sex marriage." The Supreme Court struck down DOMA because it violated both the Due Process and Equal Protection Clause of the Fourteenth Amendment. Similarly, the purpose and practical effect of FMPA is that it creates a separate status for same-sex couples and imposes a disadvantage and stigma by not being recognized under Florida law. For example the right to make health care decisions for the other spouse, without a health care directive; federal tax implications; the right to support and equitable

distribution of property obtained during the marriage; upon

the death of one spouse, the other spouse may receive an elective share of the estate; the obligation of spouses to support children of the marriage. Numerous benefits are available to married couples that form a safety net for the couples and their children that do not exist for same-sex couples at this time. See U.S. v. Windsor, 133 S. Ct. 2675 (2013). The court finds that despite the Amici Curiae assertion that there is no evidence of animus towards homosexuals by the proponents of the Florida Marriage Protection Amendment (FMPA), there is ample evidence not only historically but within the very memorandum of law filed by the Amici Curiae. For example, the affidavits of Dr. Reisman, filed by the Amici Curiae, for the proposition that, "a law encouraging homosexual behaviors appears to increase HIV risk and negative health outcomes and thus creates a danger both to the individual engaging in these behaviors as well as society as a whole." The Amici Curiae also claims that homosexuality is not the result of biology, genetics or nature, but that in fact it is a choice that is naturally subject to change and within the control of the individual. (See page 20-21 of Amici Curiae memorandum.) The Amici Curiae's memorandum paints a picture of homosexuals as HIV infected, alcohol and drug abusers, who are promiscuous and psychologically damaged and incapable of long term relationships or of raising children. (Pages 29-39). They contend, "the personal, social and financial costs of these homosexual-specific health problems concern not just those who engage in homosexual activity, but also the larger community of citizens who help provide services and who must bear part of the burden imposed by the health challenges. It is eminently rational for the voters of Florida to seek to minimize the deleterious effect of these conditions on public health, safety and welfare by affirming that marriage in Florida remains the union of one man and one woman." (Page 39). The court finds that animus has been established by the plaintiffs and that the heightened rational basis test is appropriate.

Rational Basis

Only the Amici Curiae attempts to provide a rational basis for a law that treats one class of citizens different than another. The rational bases for excluding same-sex couples from the institution of marriage, according to Amici Curiae, are to encourage procreation, a better environment for children and to preserve the traditional definition of marriage. It is worth noting that neither of the defendants in this case have argued that the basis for the FMPA is to encourage procreation or to provide a better environment for children. Only the Amici Curiae has attempted to put forward a rational basis for the unequal treatment of a segment of our society. However, Amici do not have standing to raise issues that have not been raised by the parties. Acton II v. Ft. Lauderdale Hospital, 418 So.2d 1099 (1st DCA 1982). Because the Amici Curiae are not parties to the case they may not raise different issues than the defendants. Nevertheless, for purposes of completeness the court will discuss the rational basis arguments made by the Amici Curiae. The first "rational basis" argued by the Amici Curiae is that, "FMPA" memorializes millennia of history and tradition . Justice Scalia in his dissent in Lawrence v. Texas stated, "Preserving the traditional institution of marriage ...is just a kinder way of describing the State's moral disapproval of same-sex couples," which is obviously not a legitimate purpose for the unequal treatment. In Williams v. Illinois, 399 U.S.235 (1970), the Supreme Court stated, "Neither the antiquity of a practice nor the fact of steadfast legislative and judicial adherence to it through the centuries insulates it from constitutional attack." Tradition alone cannot justify the unequal treatment of same-sex couples any more than it could justify the ban of interracial marriages, law forbidding women from voting, segregation etc. The second "rational basis" argued by the Amici Curiae is that FMPA encourages procreation. There is nothing in FMPA that encourages heterosexual couples to procreate.

Page **10** of 14

Procreation has never been a qualification for marriage. A married couple who by choice or bycircumstance do not have children is no less married than a couple that chooses to havechildren. Therefore, if the purpose of FMPA is to exclude same-sex couples from marriage, in order to encourage procreation by heterosexual couples; it fails, as "permitting same-sex couples to marry will not affect the number of opposite-sex couples who marry, divorce, cohabit, have children outside of marriage or otherwise affect the stability of opposite-sex marriages." Perry v. Schwarzenegger, 704 F. Supp.2d. 921 (N.D. Calif. 2010).

The third "rational basis" argued by the Amici Curiae is that FMPA encourages a better environment for the rearing of children. It is undisputed that the State of Florida has a legitimate interest in insuring the welfare of children. However, FMPA by limiting marriages to heterosexual couples not only fails to further the State's interest, but it in fact has the opposite effect. "(T)he only effect the marriage recognition bans have on children's well-being is harming the children of same-sex couples who are denied the protection and stability of having parents who are legally married." Obergefell v.Wymslo, 962 F.Supp.2d. 968 (S.D. Ohio 2013). The denial of marriage to same-sex couples, "(L)eads to a significant unintended and untoward consequence by limiting the resources, protections and benefits to children of same-sex parents." Pedersen v. Office of Personnel Management, 881 F.Supp.2d 294 (D. Conn. 2012). The court holds that the plaintiffs have established animus by the proponents of FMPA and that the plaintiffs have also established that there is no rational basis for the unequal treatment of homosexuals by FMPA and Florida Statute 741.04(1). The court finds Article 1, Section 27 of The Florida Constitution and Florida Statute 741.04(1) as unconstitutional under the Equal Protection Clause of the Fourteenth Amendment.

Page 11 of14

Plaintiffs Lack of Standing

The plaintiffs further move this court to declare Florida Statute 741.212(1) as unconstitutional. Florida Statute 741.212, declares that any same-sex marriage from another jurisdiction shall not be recognized by the State of Florida. The record is void of any facts establishing that the plaintiffs were married in another jurisdiction and that they have been "harmed" by Florida's failure to recognize their legal union. The motion for summary judgment holding Florida Statute 741.212 unconstitutional is denied.

Conclusion

This court is aware that the majority of voters oppose

same-sex marriage, but it is our country's proud history to protect the rights of the individual, the rights of the unpopular and the rights of the powerless, even at the cost of offending the majority. Whether it's the NRA protecting our right to bear arms when the City of Chicago attempted to ban handguns within its city limits; or when Nazi supremacists won the right to march in Skokie, Illinois a predominantly Jewish neighborhood; or when a black woman wanted to marry a white man in Virginia; or when black children wanted to go an all-white school, the Constitution guarantees and protects ALL of its citizens from government interference with those rights. All laws passed whether by the legislature or by popular support must pass the scrutiny of the United States Constitution, to do otherwise diminishes the Constitution to just a historical piece of paper.

Page 12 of14

THANKS

Jon Allen and the gracious staff of **Island House Key West** - the best gay guest house in the world – hosted my visits to Key West and allowed me to conduct interviews on their premises. Taking notes while sitting by that pool was hard work, dammit! A good portion of this book was written at **Island House Key West**.

Phil Sheldon of **HEtravel.com** – the leader in gay group travel – introduced me to the writing of **Hanns Ebensten** and guided me through his quirky material, helping me highlight the important passages.

Piero Guidugli, **Norm Kent** and **Jason Parsley** of **South Florida Gay News** (**SFGN.com**) took an avid interest in this book, publishing any sections of it that I sent them.

Fred Fejes, the acclaimed expert on gay Florida history, made himself available and generously allowed me to reframe as Q&A much of what he had written about the subject. Take brunch with Fred and all the dish is not on the table!

Dan Bready and Kevin Dickinson hosted the entire Key West contingent at their amazing home in Washington DC for the Supreme Court hearings. Without their kindness and hospitality, I doubt Aaron's idea of assembling all the plaintiffs from all the states would have materialized.

Joe Jervis, the man behind the outrageously popular **JoeMyGod.com**, had been approached by Aaron and Lee about this book. Joe suggested they speak to me about it. He also introduced me to them at **Island House**.

Stephen K. Murray-Smith, who brought me to Key West many years ago on a gay press tour, provided clarity about many aspects of contemporary gay Key West.

The Stonewall National Museum & Archives - stonewall-museum.org celebrated the victory of Huntsman and Jones in an exhibit that included an excerpt from this book. They continue to support this project. Stonewall's **Charles L. Ross** both warned me and encouraged me about the self-publishing process.

Kathy Lescoe, whom I have known since 5th grade when we competed with each other for first place in every spelling bee, copy-edited this book.

My husband, **Christopher Adams**, reviewed this project along the way, making valuable suggestions. He supplied the author's photo.

Dennis Beaver of the **Tennessee Williams Key West Exhibit – twkw.org** – gladly provided information about gay Key West history.

Nancy Kontner-Brodzki, Arlene Goldberg and **Stephen Sunday** were always willing to chat, offer help, advice and clarity about the events covered by this book.

Shannon and Joe Cubria Farris are an integral part of the Huntsman & Jones inner circle. Shannon made his photography available for the book.

Larry Blackburn and **Mark Horton** graciously supplied photography for this book.

Those interviewed and profiled in this book trusted me with very private aspects of their lives. I kept close to the recordings of those interviews, quoting them carefully while celebrating the overwhelming goodness I found in the hearts of these men and women. They each took the opportunity to review their respective chapters, making corrections and improvements whenever I may have misunderstood or misrepresented something they said. Although it will never be perfect, I hope the final product discloses my admiration for them and meets with their approval. Thank you for your courage and collaboration, **Aaron Huntsman, Lee Jones, Mark Ebenhoch, Bernadette Restivo, Susan Kent, MiKey Hudson, David Audlin, Tony Cicalese and Brian Steele.**

ABOUT THE AUTHOR

Anthony Adams divides his year between Manhattan and Fort Lauderdale. He writes primarily for the LGBT media. He is Senior Features Correspondent at *South Florida Gay News – SFGN.com* – where he has celebrated in word the best of LGBT Florida and beyond in more than 250 published pieces. He contributes to the annual *PrideLife* magazine. He wrote a play about gay priests, *A Letter From The Bishop*. He leads gay group tours in Italy and the Grand Canyon for *HEtravel.com*. He is married to his partner of 33 years, Christopher Adams.

Made in the USA
Middletown, DE
01 December 2016